A SILENT VOICE SPEAKS

The Wee Indian Woman on the Bus:
The Story of a Sikh Woman in Scotland

A Silent Voice Speaks
Trishna Singh

© Trishna Singh 2022

Published by:
Fledgling Press Ltd

Cover design by Graeme Clarke
www.graemeclarke.com

www.fledglingpress.co.uk

ISBN: 9781912280520
Printed and bound by:
Print on Demand Worldwide, Peterborough

Dedicated to the memory of all our mothers: the epitome of
shackled invisibility
And
My late husband, Harbhajan John Singh: for giving me the freedom
to break the shackles.

Foreword

My name is Trishna Singh. I am a first generation Scottish Bhat Sikh woman and this is my story.

This book is dedicated to the memories of the mothers and grandmothers of the Bhat Sikh community who lived and suffered in silence but survived against all odds. The hidden heroines who left everything in India, the land of their forefathers and mothers. They came to this strange and foreign land that they knew nothing of.

To the generation of women of the Bhat community who stood up and made a life for themselves but remained true to their heritage and culture with pride.

These are the voices of a community of women who have lived in two cultures for over half a century: unnoticed, invisible, always on the sidelines. Watching the world move on; always the observers, never the participants. Their hopes and dreams constantly stifled by internal cultural barriers that no one could see.

The survivors of an invisible oppression that suffocated their thoughts, rendering them helpless. Only being allowed to do what everyone else demanded, never what they desired.

These voices speak to you through this book. Hear them and know that they may have been your neighbours for over half a century, and you didn't get to know them...

Prologue

I wrote the following at the age of 62. I didn't have a specific readership in mind for it, it was initially just my desire, even need, to express in a few words how I felt about my childhood. But perhaps it was more than just that; what I wrote seemed to encapsulate not only my childhood but the rest of my life as well – so it's a foretaste of what this book is about.

THE WEE INDIAN WOMAN ON THE BUS

Have you ever noticed her – the wee Indian woman on the bus? Have you ever wondered who she is? Maybe you think, 'She's not been here long,' or 'These people just keep themselves to themselves.'

Well, can I tell you something? This wee woman has probably been here longer than you. She was born in the 1950s, to the first wave of people who came here from India when the British carved up their land and made them homeless refugees. She was one of the invisible children. Always on the sidelines, watching the world go by.

Everything was always out of reach. She missed out on the Beatles, Cliff Richard and Elvis Presley: she could only listen to the transistor radio when no one else was in. *The Beano*, *The Dandy* and *The Bunty* were ok, but *The Jackie* – oh no! That was out of bounds. She might be corrupted: she might start wanting the same things as the white girls! All she ever heard was, 'We don't do this, we don't do that. We are Indian.'

She wasn't allowed to dream, because dreams were for other people.

Her life centred around home and school until she was 13 when school became a distant memory, but that memory is still very clear in her mind today, 54 years later.

What does she remember? The smell of the classroom. The teacher's clear voice introducing her as, 'Our visitor from a faraway land.'

That always made her laugh! She was born in Glasgow, and the school was at the end of her street! But it was fun to pretend and, by the age of five, she was bilingual. The desire to keep learning never left her.

By the time she was 12, it began to sink in that she was different. The other girls and boys were out playing after school, going to Mission schools and Sunday schools. Sometimes she went with them and sang along to, 'Climb, climb, sunshine mountain...' But there was a slow realisation of, 'I am not like them.' Home life was like living in the village in India that her mother had fled, but never really left.

Learn to cook, learn to clean, learn to knit, sew and embroider. Learn not to ask too many questions. Life was a 'sweet prison': everything was restricted and there was no freedom to go out, no freedom to be with people her own age. She grew into a young woman in that sweet prison, but she never stopped dreaming or asking questions.

What does she remember? Not India's green fields, cool water ponds and breezes. No. Her memories are of Glasgow tenement backyards, playing *kick the can* in the street with her wee pals. Sitting at the corner of her street, pressing a penny into the hot tar. Smelling the cut grass of Richmond Park on a sunny summer's day; walking through the park from the Rutherglen Road end, with the sandpit and the swings on the left, the rockery and the big swings on the right. Best of all, she remembers walking onto the concrete bridge that links the park with Glasgow Green and the shows.

That was the best time! Every summer she was told not to go without a grown-up, but she still sneaked across the road and into the fair. She can still smell the candy floss and the toffee apples: she can still hear the noise, and the music still rings in her ears. See that wee Indian woman on the bus? She's not thinking of India: she's remembering a childhood lost to a culture that was alien – even to her.

*

I dedicated this poem to all the mothers who left their homes in the Punjab in 1948 and created new homes and lives in Scotland. These women had to leave their whole lives behind through no choice of their own, but because the British arbitrarily partitioned India. This action entirely failed to consider the enormity of what partition would cost in human life and suffering. It was visualised in an exhibition and diary produced by Sikh Sanjog, called The Daughters of the Punjab, in 2002.

MOTHER

When Mother India was torn into two. You left your
village of Galotian and Badewala
You came to Bombay, leaving behind friends, playmates,
brothers and sisters
Then separated forever when you boarded the ships and
planes to Britain.
Your mother gave you blessings, be happy in your new
life and let the gentle breezes
Bring messages of your wellbeing, the unspoken words
in your heart said we are being separated by oceans and
mother and daughter may never meet again.
You made your homes in Britain but what did you see?
What did you do? What did you enjoy?

You spent your life in a sea of nappies, cooking and cleaning, you tasted neither the freedom, the enjoyment nor the fruit of this land.

Only the men, the brothers, the husbands, the fathers reaped the fruits.

There were times when you sat together, remembering your mothers, your friends,

The fields, the spinning wheels, the cool water of the wells. And you knew that they all had become a distant dream.

In your heart was forever the desire to take your children back to your homeland.

The desire remained unfulfilled, you were caught in the money trap.

Then life takes a turn, your children are no longer children, the childhood pains and troubles are forgotten

Only to be replaced by new heartaches, and now when I think of your life

My heart fills with pain, now you are gone, leaving behind all your sorrows.

And in this life there are still unknown paths to tread

With whom do I share my heartache?

1

Roots, Childhood

My parents and grandparents came to Great Britain as economic/ refugee migrants in 1948. My father, Puran Singh Pall, and grandfather, Babu Jiwan Singh Pall, moved to the United Kingdom first (in about 1936) and my mother, Sant Ajit Kaur, and grandmother, Besant Kaur, joined them in 1948. They had been forced to leave their land and homes in the wake of the partition of India in 1947. What had been their home in Bhadewala, in the outskirts of Gujranwala, Lahore, had become Pakistan. The largest, swiftest and most violent forced migration in history.

Fourteen million people were displaced, an estimated two million killed, and as many as one million women were raped. Some women spoke of being given small packets of poison powder that, if they should be kidnapped or taken from their families by force, they should eat and die with honour, rather than be raped or abducted and forced to convert to Islam. We never heard my mother or grandmother speak of that time openly. We only heard fleeting references whilst we were growing up. As time went on and pictures would be shown on TV about refugees fleeing from some war-torn place in Africa, my mother would say, 'That's how we left our homes with the "kafla".' *(The word was mostly used in old times when people of one village or community migrated from one place to another.)* Sometimes, they would share a memory of someone giving birth in the camp or someone losing a child and then finding them again.

There was never an explicit explanation of their journey from the camps to the time of their departure to Great Britain. Always references. Sometimes my mum would say, 'The last time I saw my mother was when we were leaving.' She never explained leaving from where. Was it from the Bombay Docks? Was it from the refugee camp? Or their village? To this day, I have not read any written account of a Sikh Bhat woman's perspective on this subject. All the questions that we had no answers to, we could only surmise and piece together their history by reading other Sikh people's accounts of what took place at that time.

Sometimes I sit and in my head I have a clear line of thought of what I want to write, then it disappears. So in some ways it's best to begin at the beginning… I was born in Scotland to immigrant parents who were part refugees and part British subjects. My father had come to Great Britain in 1936 as a colonial subject. My mother joined him in 1947 as a victim of the Partition of India which had led to her home becoming Pakistan. Overnight she lost everything, including her identity.

To understand myself, I must write about my mother first. It was through watching her and how she dealt with all that happened to her that led me to where I am today. I was determined that no matter what, I would not allow myself to become a pawn in someone's hand.

My parents got married in 1935 in a small village on the outskirts of Lahore (now in Pakistan). My father left India in 1936 to travel to Great Britain for work and experience the outside world. Unfortunately for my mother, his visit lasted ten years whilst she stayed in the marital home cooking, cleaning and looking after his family. She had a baby girl who died at three months from cholera, but this was something my mother never spoke about. I only know this through conversations with other female aunts who knew my mother's life story well.

I can't imagine the trauma of living as a single woman for ten years, knowing that her husband was in a foreign country with only letters as the connection. In fact, I don't even know if my father ever wrote to my mum or if she was just included in the communications that came as general letters of wellbeing to the whole family. She never mentioned anything about that time, apart from telling me small stories of how she was treated by my paternal grandmother who was very strict and ruled the roost. My father's family consisted of five children. He had two younger sisters who both died in infancy and a brother who also died at the age of 19, of cholera. So there was only my dad, his brother and his parents. My mother also came from a family of five – three sisters and two brothers; she was the youngest of the sisters. She was very beautiful – small and petite. She had lost her father when she was only five so her eldest brother had been the father figure in her life.

*

I was born in Duke Street Hospital, Glasgow, on the 21st of October 1953, the fourth child and the third girl to come into the family. I think my parents were a little disappointed. My grandfather, however, a man of great intelligence, patience, sincerity and love, coupled with compassion for all human beings, advised them that he had already named me 'Trishna', meaning 'desire', and that I would fulfil their desire and wishes to bring good fortune and luck to the family. Indeed, this prophecy came true within the next six years, during which time my mum gave birth to three more boys, bringing our family to a grand total of four brothers and three sisters, including myself.

We lived in the Oatlands area of Glasgow – 2 Logan Street to be precise. We were the only Asian family in the area. Our house was a two-bedroomed tenement flat with no bathroom but an inside toilet, which we gradually came to realise was a luxury for some families in those days. Our home was always clean and warm. My mum could

3

speak no English at all; her whole life was spent fulfilling the needs of an extended family, from the day she got married till the day she died. She was hugely influential in shaping my thoughts and feelings, particularly my views on how the people of our community look at life. Too many within the community cannot see that we are part of the world, that we can achieve and become whatever we desire: that we were not born into this world just to do as we are told throughout our existence, we are not merely extensions of our husbands, fathers, mothers-in-law, that we are individuals in our own right. We can think! We have intelligence.

My mum was married in India and my father, who had already been to Great Britain, had returned for his marriage. They were married in 1934 or 1935 – dates and time had little meaning in the lifestyle of Indian people in those days. After the wedding, my mum came to stay with her in-laws: my father, his brother and my grandparents. This was no ordinary family. My grandfather was a much respected, well-travelled and educated gentleman. He was an astrologer and palmist to trade and he travelled to Ghana, South Africa and the UK many times before eventually settling in the UK in the late 1930s or early 40s. My grandmother was a typical village wife, not very educated but very strong-willed and also very aware of her standing in the village, being the wife of someone who was looked up to and seen as a village elder. Therefore, she commanded a great deal of respect herself. My mother, however, came from a small family and, having lost her father when she was very young, had relied on her eldest brother most of her life; she was also very close to her mother.

She was very beautiful, and when she came to my grandparents' house, people came from surrounding villages to see the beautiful bride. She was very respectful and had three things instilled in her by her mother: never refuse to do any kind of housework, never answer back, even if you are right, and always respect anybody who

4

comes to your house, whatever their age. With these teachings, my mum became well-known for her manners and genuine desire to help others without flinching from any of her duties as a daughter-in-law. My grandmother was the typical mother-in-law in that she was very dominant; she used her power over my mother, at times unfairly. Even years later, we would meet women who lived in the same village as my mum and they invariably related stories about how kind, generous and dutiful she was. My grandfather, who was seldom at home, treated her as a daughter, with respect, and showed her love as a father figure.

However, the kitchen and dealing with the daughters-in-law is the woman's place. My mother spent ten years in this environment – cooking, cleaning, caring, never asking for anything in return, no children of her own, only allowed to visit her mother when my grandmother deemed it necessary to give her some space. She spoke fondly of Maa Jennah, a Muslim lady who lived next door and had no children of her own. Maa Jennah treated my mum as her own child and would spend time with her. So many relationships lost because of partition...

It was now 1946-47, a period in history when Britain left India, having first partitioned it in an almost random fashion. Unfortunately, the former part of India that became part of Pakistan was where my father's and mother's families were from, so they became refugees. Meanwhile, my father was in the UK, living a full life with no thought of the young girl he had married and left behind. My mother's salvation was that her eldest brother was also in the UK at that point in time. He realised that my father was leading a full, rather selfish life, and had done so for the past ten years. It was apparent to my uncle that there was no intention on my father's part to be reunited with his wife. Then conflict arose; my grandmother's ticket for sailing from Bombay was later than my mum's. The crossing would take three weeks. There were arguments about how my mother, being the daughter-in-law, should have the nerve to go on a ship without any children of her own. Eventually, it was resolved by the fact that sailings could not be changed and everything had been booked and paid for by my grandfather who was in London.

My mother arrived at Tilbury Docks, Southampton, in the autumn of 1948. It must have been very cold, grey and damp. My mum used to say that the sun did not shine in her new country. She had never worn a coat, nor had she ever seen white people before. The crossing was a mammoth step for her, but coming off the ship was an even more traumatic experience. On board, she had stayed in her cabin for most of the journey. The reason for this was that she had always covered her face with the veil (purdah) in the presence of all male elders who were related to my father.

Even though there were quite a lot of families on the ship from the same region as her, she felt alone. These other people, some had children, or their husbands, mothers or mothers-in-law with them. She was completely alone, going to stay with a husband whom she had not seen for ten years. They stayed for a few months in London, then moved to Liverpool. It was at this point that my uncle realised that my father should be made to part company with the group he was socialising with; they were a bad influence and my mother was constantly being left at home on her own.

There is not a lot I can say about my mum's life at this time because she chose not to talk about it. And as we were growing up, we were too naïve to even think about asking her about this period of her life. It truly is only now, when she has been gone for 36 years, that I am wishing that I had spoken to her, asked her questions about it. But it is, of course, too late now. I can only imagine the pain and mental anguish that she must have gone through at that time.

My parents moved to Glasgow in 1949, and my eldest sister,

Sukhwant, was born in Rotten Row Hospital in that year, followed a year later by my brother, Gurdev. My sister, Ashan, was born at home in Maryhill in 1952. My parents then bought their own house in Logan Street, Oatlands. I was born in Duke Street Hospital in 1953. My younger brother, Subash, was born at home in 1955, my next brother, Gadraj, born in 1957, and my youngest brother, Chander, was born in 1959.

My second-youngest brother was only 40 days old when my mother received a letter informing her that her mother had died in India. She was devastated by the news but received only the minimum of care and support from my grandmother. Having no daughters of her own, I think my gran found it very difficult to show any real feelings towards my mum. Throughout this time, my father was working as a door-to-door salesman, selling clothes and rugs; this involved travelling to towns and cities such as Aberdeen, Perth, Falkirk, Stonehaven and Greenock, which meant that he would sometimes be away for one or two weeks at a time.

My dad had enlisted, in 1944, in the Royal Pioneer Corps, British Reserves, Bradford. His time in the army greatly affected his behaviour for the rest of his life. He was very strict: shoes had to be polished until you could see your face in them, the bedtime routine involved making sure everybody was in bed, lights out, no socks to be worn in bed. He would actually lift the covers to see if we had our socks off! He was not going to let any of his children grow up to be namby-pamby softies.

In hindsight, this strictness stood us all in good stead. We all still make sure we have polished shoes. And as for my brothers, it was always suit, tie, shirt, handkerchief; these, he would say, were the signs of a gentleman! He himself dressed very smartly at all times and the blazer was a firm favourite of his.

When I got married, my husband was a very smart dresser but he didn't really bother much about his shoes. So it became my mission to show this man that polished shoes were essential as a finishing touch. I went out and bought shoe polish and a brush set. It became an integral part of my husband's dress routine after that, even if it meant me polishing his shoes!

We lived in the Oatlands house until 1963 or 64. During this time we spent many happy, carefree days at Wolseley Street Primary School. Our school was just across the road from our house, and I remember my first day at school. My dad took me in to Mrs. Brown's class. At playtime, I decided I'd learned enough and walked out of school, straight home. Unfortunately, this was short-lived and I came to understand that this was not on. However, school was fun, the teachers were nice and we had many friends.

A couple of teachers remain in my mind. Firstly, Miss Eyre, who wore green overalls and a hat made of feathers. She was very strict, but when I think now of her manner, she would probably be deemed racist in today's society. As children, we all thought Mrs. Nelson was a man dressed up as a woman. This is probably because she had short hair, unlike the fashion at the time, and strode up and down the classroom with her hands clasped behind her back. She assumed we had come from India and treated us with great respect, as though we were fragile china. We, of course, lapped this up.

I remember many events from my childhood in Glasgow, but one that sticks out is the time when I was five years old: my father, who had been drinking the night before, had really bad heartburn. All of us children were still in bed and he asked for someone to go across the road to McDonald's sweet shop for some Rennies. Everybody kept shtum except me, so I got up, got dressed and went to the shop. Coming out of the shop, I failed to see a cyclist come speeding round the corner; he knocked me down. I remember it so well. All of a sudden there was a crowd gathered around me and I could hear people asking, 'Who is she? Does anyone know her?' Then someone broke through the crowd. It was Bob, a wee Scottish man who had befriended our family and was our very own painter and decorator. Bob always wore a bunnet.

He picked me up and started to walk towards our house, then there was this wild shriek – it was my grandmother. She had been on a trip to Doncaster and had just got off the bus on her return. She started wailing and screaming, 'Who sent you to the shop? Why are you out at this time? Oh my God, her leg's broken! She's scarred for life! She will have a limp! No one will marry her!' Remember, I was only five years old at the time. Then Granny decides to stop Bob midway up the stairs to question me.

'Who sent you out at this time and why?'

So I told her I went for Rennies because Dad had heartburn. That was it, off she went again, calling her son all the names under the sun, cursing his drinking habits. My grandmother was mortified that my leg had been broken. I was in a stookie for three months and I remember being pushed around in a pram by my sisters. As far as my granny was concerned, I might be damaged for the rest of my life. Once the plaster was removed she started to massage olive oil on my leg on a daily basis for at least three months. This, she maintained, encouraged the healing process and prevented me from having a limp. I had been saved.

We had many white friends and we joined in their games and fights – the 'big backs' versus the 'wee backs' ('backs' was the word given to the backyards of tenement closes). Some names still remain in my memory: my best friend was Isabel Innes – she lived across from the 'hot baths' and went to the Catholic school. Then there was Kay Bishop who was at my primary school also, but remains in my mind because of how tall she was. Our neighbours, who lived next door to us, were the Carmichael family. They were very quiet and had only one child but were lovely to us. Sometimes we would knock on their door for something, but really just to peek inside their house which looked like something we'd see on the telly.

Next to our house in Logan Street, on the corner, was the newsagent's shop, run by Mr. McGregor. We called him 'McGreegor'. He would be termed nowadays as a complete racist – he disliked us with a vengeance. We were not allowed into his shop or anywhere near his newspaper stand that stood outside. What we did do was play ball against his wall that faced onto our side of the street. This drove him crazy, the constant thudding of tennis balls against his wall. We would be singing – more like screeching – the rhymes, 'Over the garden wall, ah let ma baby fall, my mother came oot and gave me cloot, over the garden wall'. Or, 'Up in Aberdeen, there lives a fairy queen, esha asha, you're a wee smasha, up in Aberdeen'. And this one that always stays in my head even now, 'Rabbie Burns wis born in Ayr and noo he's doon at the Georges Square, an' if you want to see him there, just jump oan the bus and pay your fare!'

There was also 'the dunny' that belonged to McGreegor. Dunny was short for what we called the dungeon, or basement in the tenements. There was a stone staircase that led to this and there was a kind of storage unit with a big wooden door where McGreegor stored his shop goods.

We thought he stored kids that he had murdered in it! All the kids in the stair and a few stairs along were petrified of him. He was a very big man, probably about six feet tall and very broad, with glasses and a big loud voice. When he shouted we all scattered. We lived quite dangerously at times… The dunny steps led out to the backs of the tenements and there was a big gap. There were windows that had bars on them so we would climb onto the side window and step onto the window that faced the steps and we would jump across the gap. There were two jumps – the wee jump and the big jump. The wee jump was when you just stood on the bottom sill of the barred window and jumped. The big jump was when you actually climbed the bars onto the second strap of the iron bars, and then jumped. It was a miracle that no one fell through the gap and broke their bones, there were plenty of near misses. We survived our childhood adventures and they are very happy memories of a time that has now sadly disappeared.

Enoch Powell 'Rivers of Blood Speech'

When Enoch Powell made that speech we had no idea of what it meant, nor the implications. We lived happily in our own wee world. We would hear the stories of what was happening in England but it didn't bear any kind of meaning to our lives. When we heard that a new bill was being passed that meant repatriation for all immigrants, we thought it was hilarious. We would annoy our cousins who had come from India in the late 50s, early 60s – 'That's it, pal, you're goin' hame! We wur born here, he's not talking about us!'

It was a while before we were to understand the terrible implications his intentions would have had on everyone and everything in our lives.

The Stoddard family lived on the ground floor flat in the tenement next to our 'close'. There were about ten of them in that family, mainly boys, if memory serves correctly. One Halloween, we were all dressed up to go out guising. My sister had put on my uncle's suit and trilby hat and was standing on the landing, waiting for us to come down. All of a sudden there was this shouting, 'Hey, Shuggie, is that you?'

Well, we couldn't run fast enough and my sister was engulfed by a group of boys who thought she was Shuggie Stoddard. Then there was Mr. Smellie, who lived on the first landing of our tenement and was one of those stiff-upper-lip men who had probably fought in the war. Always immaculately dressed, with his bunnet on his head and a fine whiskery moustache. His door was always polished and the nameplate shone – you could see your face in it. He remains in my memory because we knew he didn't like brown people. He despised us and would always make some grumpy remark if he saw us going up and down the stairs. Some things happen to you in childhood that remain in your mind forever.

I remember my grandfather sitting at his writing bureau, and sitting in his lap listening to his stories about Africa. Cuddling up to him in his bed and eating porridge with lashings of fresh butter swimming in it. Looking out of my grandad's top flat window and hearing the screams of people on the rides at the Glasgow Green fun fair.

Richmond Park was our daily haunt: climbing the trees, having picnics and crossing the bridge to go to the fair. Summer holidays were great times. Every Saturday, we would pack a picnic and set off to visit the Campsie Hills. We would get as far as Polmadie Road, then check the time with a passer-by and return home because it was tea-time. We never did get to the Campsie Hills.

Oatlands people were working-class: genuine, down-to-earth and with real hearts. We went shopping for the old women who lived alone, knocked on doors and ran away, and held concerts on the stair landings where you paid to attend with 'wallies' – broken pieces of china. We lived opposite Richmond Park, on the other side of Glasgow Green. To me, it was a magical place where, each summer holiday, the 'shows' would arrive.

I was fascinated by the caravans, with their beautiful lace curtains and lanterns hanging outside. Looking up the steps, you could see inside where there were vases of flowers on the tables, bright rugs and cushions on the sofas. To a seven-year-old girl it was magical, watching the gypsy women with their big skirts and earrings, and the handsome gypsy boys, who always winked when you walked past. My parents would take us on one supervised visit to the shows and we were allowed on the safe rides – the swings and roundabouts. Waltzers, motorbikes and the Big Wheel were forbidden because the gypsy boys stood at the back of the Waltzers and swung the cars round as they speeded up. They swaggered about, chatting up the girls. We were warned not to go to the shows on our own and told that the gypsies would take us away and make us work like slaves in their camps. But we never listened and sneaked across, through the park and over the bridge, on to the Green to explore the shows.

All the latest music blared out from the roundabouts, swings, Waltzers, the Big Wheel and the helter-skelter. The sweet smell of candy floss and toffee apples and the screams of the girls on the Big Wheel with their boyfriends made me want to be white too, like them – why couldn't I go on the Big Wheel and stay out late? I used to dream of being kidnapped by the gypsies so I could work the stalls in big earrings and skirts that made me want to dance. But no one kidnapped me, and every year the shows would come and go with no change in my lifestyle.

My grandfather died in 1960 of a cancer-related illness. On the day of his funeral, I remember getting up and going to my friend Isabel's house to go to school. When I arrived there, I burst into tears; her mum comforted me and took me back home. We children were mostly left to deal with these things on our own. Talking to each other about what was happening or going on. A great many people attended my grandfather's funeral – he was a great loss to all of us. He had had great hopes for all his grandchildren, especially his three granddaughters who were going to become doctors, nurses, lawyers, anything that they wanted.

After he died, my grandmother stayed with us, or with my dad's younger brother, our Chacha (this was the title of Dad's younger brother, rather than uncle) Joginder. Chacha had seven sons and two daughters – we were, and still are, very close to my cousins. We all spent many happy hours together as they were all younger than me and my sisters. To this day they still address us as Vuddee Bhen Ji (big sister). There would always be a fight about who was going to sleep with Granny. We all knew that if you slept with Dadhi, she would rub your legs and the small of your back. She would be awake at the crack of dawn and recite her *Japji Sahib*, the morning prayer for Sikhs. Then she would make Indian tea with spices, and rather than toast, she was very fond of Jacob's Cream Crackers and would put an inch of proper fresh butter on them. Whoever slept beside Dadhi had this treat to look forward to.

For me, it was the beginning of my spiritual journey. As I listened to the 'patt' (prayer), it gave me a sense of peace even though I didn't understand a word of what she was reciting. I didn't know it then, but as time went on and I began to read the *Japji Sahib* patt myself, the memory of Dadhi's voice would come to me.

*

We moved to a bigger house in Pollokshields, 103 McCulloch Street, to be precise, around 1964 and all our lives began to change. We started to grow up and become aware of the great differences in our way of life compared to that of our friends whom we left behind in the Oatlands. We were no longer allowed to muck about with boys and girls and, gradually, boys became a complete no-no in any of our activities, apart from our own cousins and brothers.

School was now Melville Street Primary, a big change from our cosy set up at Wolseley Street. At the new school there were more Asians, in particular, Pakistani children whose parents were in the middle-class bracket. These kids wore school uniforms. We girls were not allowed to because we couldn't wear skirts.

This was, in my memory, the first major religious issue in my life. Both dress and religion would become obstacles for me in later years. Other things that were deemed inappropriate for us to do, and which were banned in the name of religion, were swimming, dancing, school trips and accessing any kind of outside entertainment unless we were accompanied by our parents. We were not allowed to take part in the school dances as we would be dancing with boys, but in the lead up to dances we would have practices, and I remember I would always be partnered with a Jewish girl called Judith. She was very tall and had red hair. I think she also felt out of place and so together we would practice the Gay Gordon's and the Military Two Step. When it actually came to the day of the school dance, we would both be very conveniently ill… No teacher ever questioned this or even attempted to understand why. Melville Street School was full of children from different backgrounds to us and what we had grown up with in Oatlands. In hindsight, knowing what we now know about covert racism and discrimination, the school was full of this type of behaviour. But we were so naive and unworldly, we had no idea. We assumed it was all our fault because our parents didn't let us join in with all the activities.

Every Friday, I and two of my cousins had a wee ritual. We would stand outside the school gates, clasp both hands together, prayer-style, and utter the words, 'Thank God we don't have to be here for two days!' Then we would walk home.

My dad became very active in various organisations in Pollokshields, including the Indian Workers' Association, the Indian Film Association and Sikh Gurdwara. He was an interpreter also, called upon to interpret for men newly arriving from India.

Extract from my dad's diary

March 1971: We, and students and 30 other immigrants took part in a rally from Glasgow University to Strathclyde University.

Our lives came to revolve around his meetings, which were often arranged at the drop of a hat. A phone call to say he had invited ten to twenty men to the house, to get things organised. And my mother, working on her tight budget, had to make a spread fit for a king materialise, basically out of thin air. There were no freezers then and our fridge was a novelty at the time. In actual fact, most of these meetings ended up as drinking soirees or punch-ups.

Working door-to-door, as my dad did, was hard, and in those days, there was no other employment for the men in our community that they felt was open to them. They were far from home and faced with a growing awareness that their bridges were burnt; there was no prospect of a return to the life they had left behind. Their dreams of a land where the streets were paved with gold were crumbling and the reality of what the future held was dawning on them. But, when the hangover had gone and the apologies had been made to family and cronies, then life would go back to normal – until the next time.

As I got older, I realised that the way of life these men had left behind was of working hard and drinking hard; that was the Punjabi culture. It prompted me to say, 'All the Sikh men who came from that particular Punjabi culture and found themselves in Scotland would have been in their seventh heaven. A pub on each corner! Who could ask for more?'

When I was 12 or thereabouts, I had several discussions with my father on various matters. One topic that stands out in my mind was when, at 9 a.m. on Sunday 10 October 1965, *Apna Hi Ghar Samajhiye*, or *Make Yourself at Home*, began broadcasting on BBC television and radio. Its target audiences were recent immigrants into the UK from India and Pakistan. Hugh Carlton-Greene, the then BBC director-general, had commissioned the series after concluding that the BBC was neither talking to the newest British citizens nor doing a great deal to combat rising racial prejudice.

The programme had Jim Callaghan on once and Margaret Thatcher twice; it acquired political muscle and clout. It provided a 'vote bank' of immigrants. Their proud boast was that 'No other minority programme could claim to have got prime ministers on to the show.'

One politician, however, never accepted his invitation onto the programme. Namely Enoch Powell, the Conservative MP whose Rivers of Blood speech in 1968 infamously warned against further immigration.

At a lunch meeting, he was once asked by the presenter of *Make Yourself at Home,* 'Mr. Powell, why don't you take part in our programme?' And he said, 'As an MP, I have to advise my own people first.' The presenter replied, 'Aren't our audience now your people too?' The series ran for 14 years.

Contributors spoke a combination of Hindi, Urdu and English, providing informal language lessons based around everyday situations encountered in the UK. Entertainment was provided by a range of Indian, classical or Bollywood music. It was introduced in the *Radio Times* by producer, David Gretton, who heralded 'a new field of public service broadcasting.'

The sole English contribution came from Maurice Foley, a junior government minister. With classic Whitehall understatement, he said, 'In the world of today, we all need to know a great deal more about each other.'

Various contributors explained the miracle of modern gas boilers; the bureaucratic necessity of the NHS registration card; the inside story of a polling booth and so on. In addition, there was a programme slot aimed at teaching 'us' English. This usually involved discussing general household and social situations and a typical scene went like this:

'This is a switch on the wall. A switch. This is a light. A light. If I turn on the switch, the light will come on.'

For us first generation Asians, this was hysterically funny. We would be rolling about laughing our heads off. We had been born here so we spoke pure Glaswegian, Leeds, Brummie, whatever our birthplace was. Listening to the upper-crust, cut-crystal English being taught to us on television seemed so totally out of place. Another slot on the same programme was 'the interview', and famous people invited to this included Asian women.

My dad was always highly complimentary about how well they spoke and how educated they were. This annoyed me, and one Sunday morning, I said to Dad, 'So why are women like Mum and other Bhat women still covering their faces with the veil? Why are they not encouraged to go on telly? You know what, Dad? I think this is a real bitch of a community!'

Now, at that time I was only 12 and I didn't really know how bad or rude that was. Furthermore, the word 'bitch' translated into Punjabi is not nice. My dad was really angry at this and, to add salt to the wound, I was also reprimanded by my mum and told to keep my mouth shut in future. But that incident actually sparked my resolve to make sure I was going to do something with my life. I decided there and then that I would be the first Bhat woman on television. And I was!

In the early 90s, I appeared in an STV programme filmed at the Gateway Studios in Edinburgh. I was working with Sikh Sanjog and was invited to take part, which made me the first Bhat woman on television in the UK. I remember asking my friend and neighbour, Margaret Kinghorn, to accompany me as I was very nervous of going on my own.

The programme was called '100 Scottish Women' and was hosted by Kaye Adams. Each week a variety of issues were discussed. The week that I was in the audience, we were discussing advertising and how it related to the ordinary woman on the street.

I was sitting in the audience and started chatting to the woman sitting next to me. She was asking me if I was going to ask any questions of the panel and I said, 'Yes, I'm so annoyed that people of colour are never shown in any adverts. We buy Fairy Washing Up Liquid, Kellogg's Cornflakes and all the other stuff that is shown on telly.'

She was quite taken aback and then said, 'I am on the panel and I'll be answering the question. Are you really going to ask?' I confirmed to her I would.

I think the fact that she was worried about me asking made me want to do it more!

So I asked the question and the camera was on me. I was slightly daunted but not too much. Sadly, nothing came of my question until about 15-20 years later when we started seeing a gradual influx of people of colour being included in ads.

I think that if my dad had been alive, he would have been proud, not angry, but my mum would have been mortified.

*

In 1968 my sister was married into a family in Edinburgh. The father of the family had died in a tragic car accident a couple of years earlier. This family consisted of six brothers, two sisters, a mother and grandmother. My sister was two weeks away from her 18th birthday when she was married. Little did I know at the time that my sister's marriage would change my life, both then and at a much later stage.

The first major change happened instantly. I was taken out of school that summer, at the age of thirteen. When we had been making the transition from primary to secondary school, my teacher, Miss McTavish, had been horrified at my decision to go to Kinning Park Secondary School instead of Bellahouston Academy. She was so annoyed with me.

I remember her standing in front of me and saying, 'Why are you throwing away such an opportunity?'

I just stood there and said, 'I am going to Kinning Park, Miss, because all my friends are going there.'

She was just so angry on my behalf and I would fully understand her anger quicker than I thought. I was at Kinning Park Secondary School for 18 months. At the end of the first term at secondary school, we were given our exam marks and I was awarded the Prize for Excellence in all subjects. For the remaining two terms running, I was being pushed by my teachers to change from a 'C' class to an 'S' class. The difference between the two was that the C class was for commercial teaching and the S class was for academic study. I didn't take that up and stayed in my C class.

Then disaster struck. My dad contacted the school and said that I had gone to India to visit my grandmother and would come back to school on my return from India. Immigrants in the 60s were still considered 'new' to the country and the school believed my dad's story. In actual fact what had happened was that some girls from the Bhat community had run away from home in Manchester. They had been on the verge of arranged marriages and had run away with white boys. This news spread like wildfire throughout the community and people were literally petrified that the same might happen to their family. Decisions were taken across the whole of the UK by Bhat parents, and so many girls were taken out of school under the false pretence of visiting India. No discussion, no explanations, that was it. I was devastated. I loved school and had dreams of somehow, magically, going to university.

At this point in time there was a School Board Inspector who was linked to the schools in the area. I can't remember her name but she remains in my memory. She would come to the house with her clipboard and paper and a list of all pupils who had been off school for a period of time without explanation. My younger brothers attended Bellahouston Academy and she would come to check on them if they had been off. At the bottom of her list was my name, Trishna Devi Pall.

She would ask the same question each time she had reason to call at our house: 'Is Trishna back from India?' and I would say, as I had been instructed by my parents to say, 'No, not yet but when she comes back, she will come to school.'

I would slam the door shut and jump up and down, calling her all the names under the sun. Couldn't she see me? I was standing right in front of her! Was she blind?

On one occasion after I had 'left' school, I had a small cyst appear on my ankle. The doctor suggested to my parents that I get it surgically removed. Once I had been discharged from hospital, after my very small operation, I was still bandaged up and resting. There was a knock on the door and my dad opened it to two men dressed in overcoats, trilby hats and with papers to search the property. They were CID, looking for two seamen who had jumped ship and they had been checking the hospitals for anyone with a foreign name. My name had come up. I, on the other hand, was in my bed thinking, 'They've come at last. It's the school, they have sent the police to get me back to school!'

Sadly, they believed my father when he produced my birth certificate and proved that I was his daughter and not a foreign seaman. My dreams of returning to school were crushed forever.

Our lives continued in much the same pattern. My brothers were now growing up and my eldest brother had started to work. My father was interested in educating him, but I think that the fact he could be earning money outweighed all other arguments. My brother was duly dispatched to Aberdeen to stay with my mum's brother and, maybe, learn the door-to-door trade. Door-to-door salesmanship was not for my brother, Gurdev, and he quickly moved on to work for Glasgow Corporation buses. He worked in a number of sectors before settling into work with Glasgow City Council Social Work. He is now a Retirement Housing Manager in Glasgow, where he still lives.

My younger brother, Subash, joined the Govan shipyards as an apprentice joiner and then went on to become involved in the Arts. He was instrumental in creating the first Asian Radio station in Glasgow – Kranti Radio. Amongst other things, he appeared in small parts in the film, *The Big Man*, alongside Billy Connelly and Liam Neeson and a Bollywood film, *Udham Singh*. He now lives in Manchester and is still involved in the creative arts.

Gadraj left school and was sent to Manchester to stay with my dad's cousin, who had a thriving corner shop, to learn the trade of shopkeeper. It was not long before he came back much wiser and very knowledgeable about being a shopkeeper. He went on to work with British Rail as a guard. He now works with NHS England and has been living in Birmingham for over 20 years.

Chander, the youngest, left school and joined a printers as an apprentice and that became his trade. He now works as a self-employed courier driver. He moved from Glasgow to East Kilbride 25 years ago and still lives there.

Aberdeen holds many happy memories for me. My mum's younger brother, Ajager Singh, lived there on his own because his wife and kids were still in India. Between 1958 and 1967, we spent practically every summer holiday in Aberdeen. We would pack ourselves into the back of our Ford van, first putting down a mattress in the back to make a proper space for the seven of us to sit. The suitcases would also be loaded up. Dinner would be packed and we would leave Glasgow at seven o'clock in the morning. While my dad drove, we in the back would tell jokes, eat our sweets, count the cars behind, wave to people or sleep. We always arrived in Aberdeen about eight or nine o'clock at night. After unloading, we just went to sleep. And the men sat and ate and drank. My mum would cook the food and then join us for a sleep.

Aberdeen was our main holiday. We would visit the permanent fun fair practically every day, walking up Urquhart Road with our sweets and bags. In the morning we would go to the bakery at the corner of Urquhart Road for hot Aberdeen rolls, half-a-penny each. The taste was like butter melting in your mouth. We would dip them in hot tea while sitting and watching Andy Stewart's White Heather Club. Life was simple, uncomplicated. We all had our dreams, not knowing where our lives were going or what traumas were ahead.

We would sometimes stay longer in Aberdeen than the school holidays lasted, so we would go to school there too. The local school was a Catholic school in Nelson Street, and we even learnt the Hail Mary and other prayers. Aberdeen was like fairyland to us. In the winter, the snow would be knee-deep and we would have snowball fights, build snowmen and go from my uncle's house in Nelson Lane to our cousins' (my mum's sister's son's) house in Nelson Place, sliding through people's stairs. The stairs and closes of houses in Aberdeen were made of highly polished wood, so our shoes would come off and we would imagine ourselves to be ice skaters. We'd play in the gardens and climb over the railway track for rhubarb and amongst all this, I had my dreams of being an actress, air hostess, lawyer or even doctor. I had no idea how I was going to even attempt to achieve these impossible goals, but those were my dreams and I longed for night to fall when I could lie in bed in peace and dream away.

Reading books kept us going, and at school we had access to library books and were also allowed to go to the local library. Enid Blyton's *The Secret Seven* and *The Famous Five*, Louisa M. Alcott's *Little Women*, *Cherry Ames Flight Nurse* and *Anne of Green Gables* were just a few of my favourite reads. My passion for reading never stopped. I think that's what kept my mind stimulated, always being the imaginary heroine of these stories. As we got older, my sisters and I would secretly buy magazines like *Red Letter, Jackie* and *Secrets*. These we would read, then duly burn before my parents were able to see them. Comics like *The Judy, The Bunty, The Dandy, The Beano, Beezer* and *Topper* were all ok; even my dad would pick these up for us when he went to buy his *Daily Record*, which we were also allowed to read. The holidays in Aberdeen slowly stopped when my uncle and his family moved to Glasgow in the late 60s. And so now we are back at the previous point mentioned, concerning my sister's marriage in 1968.

She moved to Edinburgh and seemed quite happy. She never discussed in any great detail her new life, especially where her husband was concerned. It was fun, she said. She had left one large family and joined another large family. I suppose it was a million miles away from our daily routine of impromptu parties hosted by my father that mostly ended up in a riot of some kind.

By 1970 we were beginning to prepare for my brother's wedding – getting the house decorated and put in order for the great occasion. My father was the eldest male in his family but had left it very late in having children. Everybody was over the moon that now, at this late stage, his son was to be married. My grandmother, who was now in her eighties and quite ill, also looked forward to the great day. And for my mother, on one hand there was happiness but on the other, great stress and strain around the finances.

My brother married a girl from Glasgow, from a family that we knew well. In fact, I had gone to school with my sister-in-law, Ravinder. The only thing was, I knew she was engaged to my brother whereas she did not. This, in turn, indirectly takes me back to my eldest sister's wedding.

I had been told to go round to my brother's future in-laws with some sweetmeats. This was July 1967 or 68, the season of the Orange Walks. So there I was, sitting on the number 68 bus going towards Paisley Road West when the Orange Walk went past. The bus was held up for one and a half hours as they went past with their banners and bands and all. When I got to my sister-in-law-to-be's house, she opened the door, took one look at me and slammed the door in my face. She had just found out that I was to be her sister-in-law. She and I had been really close schoolfriends, so she felt I had duped her. I left the sweetmeats and returned on the 68 bus feeling quite bad.

My brother's wedding took place despite this. It even made the papers, the *Daily Record* to be precise. He was quoted as saying that he was very happy with the choice and looked forward to seeing his new bride. In fact, he didn't really say anything because he wasn't allowed to. The wedding went well and I did my first real dance and sang songs that I had learned from my brother's Indian records. My sister and I were determined to show our relatives what was what. Mainly the female contingent of my mum's side of the family, who thought we were British-born imbeciles who didn't know anything about India or its culture, who couldn't speak Punjabi properly, a first generation of British-born Sikhs! Well, we showed them good and proper. My dance routine, *Bindiya chamkegi* from the film, *Do Raaste*, was such a success that, 50 years on, people still ask me to do my party piece!

After the wedding, there were lots of ups and downs in the family. My father continued being involved in the Gurdwara committees. Bringing home people at the drop of a hat and expecting three-course meals to come from nowhere. My mum was always worrying about how we could afford to continue in this way.

My sister got married in 1972 in our house at 103 McCulloch Street and then my dad decided we should move, so we sold up and moved along the street to number 40, which was a big change: from the ground floor to the top floor tenement. Also, No. 40 was bigger and had an upstairs as well. It was a lovely house which faced a bowling green. I spent many a night looking out of my attic bedroom window, wondering if I would ever get married.

Sadly, No. 40 and some other houses in McCulloch Street have since been demolished, although the bowling green and 103 is still there. Personally, my life was so restricted there were times when I felt I would suffocate. My only outlet was my imagination and I would let it run wild. My thoughts were always centred around this wonderful freedom I thought I was going to get when I got married.

I was nearly 19 years old now and all my friends were married; some of them even had one or two children. I read books to pass my time, cooked, sewed, listened to Indian music and read as much Punjabi as I could. I also went shopping with my sister-in-law, who was so quiet there were times when I thought I would scream if I didn't have someone to talk to. We didn't have a phone in our house but our neighbour downstairs, Mrs. McColl, allowed us to take phone calls in her house. Mrs. McColl lived with her daughter, who was a few years older than me. Often, on the pretext of going to get a phone message from her, or if my sisters had phoned and Mrs. McColl had given us a shout to let us know, I would go and sit with her and her daughter just for the sheer pleasure of having someone to talk to – especially Mrs. McColl, because I felt more comfortable talking to an older person about my restricted life.

I built what I thought my life might be like on what I saw and read about in Indian films. My husband was going to be a handsome hero who fell madly in love with me, serenaded me with romantic love songs, whisked me off my feet, took me out on romantic weekends and wined me and dined me! All my fantasies rolled into one. They did come true, to a certain extent, but they were peppered with the most difficult and extreme situations that have made me who I am today.

2

The Sikh Faith

I have written this chapter as a form of primer, really, into the Sikh faith, customs and traditions, because I've found that many westerners are blissfully unaware of what makes Sikhs do what they do, be what they are. So this chapter should, I hope, put into context what follows on in this book. It should be noted, however, that Sikhism is an evolving culture, subject to western influences, and that what applied to my generation of young people in the 1950s and 60s does not apply to the same extent now, in the 21st century.

The founder of Sikhism was the 15th century Guru Nanak, whose mission was to enlighten his followers by making them look at themselves as individuals and equals. At that time, class divisions and a layered societal structure were being taught by the Hindu (Brahmins) and Muslim (Maulvi) priests. They stated that their path was the only true way to God. To attain this, the Muslim rulers used conversion by force, whilst the Hindus used the caste system.

People who became Sikhs (disciples or followers of Guru Nanak's path) were often low caste Hindus – lepers, untouchables or people who felt they could not relate to religion because they were uneducated. By following Guru Nanak's path of simple devotion and prayer and looking within themselves to find peace and to help one another, a new religious path opened up for them.

Sikhs are defined by their religion and Sikhism is a way of life. It teaches us to respect all humankind, as given by the words of

Guru Gobind Singh, the last living Guru of the Sikhs: 'All human beings are the same, there is no distinction between one and another, no caste, no creed and no religion. The spirit of God prevails in all human beings.'

All books on Sikhism maintain Guru Nanak's message that everyone is equal and that there should not be any divide or caste system within the Sikh way of life. But, in practice, Sikh festivals do exhibit differences depending on the community involved, which part of India the ancestors of that community came from, and how rural or urban the lifestyles of those ancestors were.

Sikhism is a practical religion – a faith of hope and optimism. Its ideals form a large part of the more progressive elements in humanity today. It shows mankind how to lead a worthy and useful life in the world, which elevates it into the status of Universal World Faith.

Sikhs practice Simran (meditation), Seva (service) and Sangat (congregation) in the pursuit of leading a happy, healthy, holy, honest and humble life, and ultimately the achievement of spiritual union of their Atma (soul) with Parmatma (God).

Sikhism teaches respect for individuals and love for one's neighbours. It teaches how to be useful in society, how to care for the interests and concerns of others and cherish the values taught by the Gurus. Social commitment and goodwill among Sikhs have inspired them to finance and undertake projects of social benefit because of their belief that human beings all over the world form just one family, the family of humans, namely Manas-ki-jaat. This concept is reflected in Ardas, the daily prayer, which ends:

Nanak Nam Chardi Kala Tere Bhane Sarbat Ka Bhalla – O Almighty God, kindly shower your blessings on the entire humanity.

*

I made myself a promise at the age of five that I would one day learn to read and write this strange language of my parents and sit on the podium and read from the Guru Granth Sahib. By the age of 13, I had learned the basics of Gurmukhi (the written word of the Sikhs) and could read letters that came from India for my mother. My mother thought it strange that her daughter, who had never set foot in India, wanted, and was able to, read from the Holy Scriptures. My mum first started me on the *Sunder Gutka*, which is the compilation of all Sikh morning and evening prayers; I would read these and my mum would listen.

The whole thing about being Sikh began to hold a different meaning for me at this time. As a young girl growing up in Glasgow, I found that my non-Sikh friends were making plans to go to college, socialise, work, talk about their aspirations for life. Whereas we were being taught everything that would make us good wives, daughters-in-law, mothers and eventually mothers-in-law: we were being home-schooled in cooking, sewing, knitting, embroidery.

Our route through life was being mapped out by our parents and we had no say in any aspect of this planning. My perception of being Sikh was becoming very 'coloured'. I began to detest this religion. Why were we not allowed freedom of choice? Why couldn't we go out and mix with other teenagers? Who made this religion that was holding me back from my dreams? But I was too scared to voice these questions or, when I did occasionally pluck up the courage to ask, I would be told that that was the way it was and that was it. No explanation was ever offered.

Yet all the while, I prayed for God to show me the way. There must be more to this life than cooking, cleaning and forever being told by others what to do, I asked Him. I had still to reach the point of understanding that Guru Nanak, the founder of Sikhism, had embedded in his writings, that there must be equality for women. In fact, he was the first male of his time to challenge the oppression of women in India. He wrote:

> From woman, man is born;
>
> Within woman, man is conceived;
>
> To woman he is engaged and married.
>
> Woman becomes his friend;
>
> Through woman, the future generations come.
>
> When his woman dies, he seeks another woman;
>
> To woman he is bound.

So why call her bad? From woman, woman is born; without woman, there would be no one at all.

WOMEN IN SIKHISM

Sikhism has given full religious, social and political rights to women. They can lead religious congregations, take part in the continuous recitation of the Holy Scriptures and work as a priest or preacher. Sikh women have a birthright to attend all occasions of public worship, all social functions and political conferences. In fact, Sikh women have been at the forefront in every walk of life.

The accepted beliefs and moral standards of the family and the community are taken for granted and they are not subjects for questioning or discussion. However, with the arrival of fourth and fifth generations of Sikhs being born in the U.K., communities have, of necessity, adapted and evolved.

Sikh history also furnishes many examples of women who inspired men to heroic deeds, such as Mai Bhago, the first Sikh woman warrior whose story inspired me when I eventually read it. 'In the year 1705, the legend goes, during a great battle against an empire, 40 soldiers abandoned their post and returned to their villages. Mai Bhago turned to them and said, 'You will not abandon the fight. You will return to the fire, and I will lead you.'

She donned a turban, mounted a horse and, with a sword in her hand and fire in her eyes, she led them to where no one else would. In the story, the 40 deserters who followed Mai Bhago back into the battlefield all died. They fought for a future they did not live to see. They did not know that they would be remembered or that their fight would make a difference. They did not know that our people would go on to live in every part of the world and recite their names in the *Ardas,* the prayer read at the end of every Sikh prayer service and sermon, whether at home on your own or with the *sangat* (congregation). Today, we call the 40 warriors the *Chali Muktey – the Forty Liberated Ones,* not because they were liberated in death but because they were liberated in life.

For the warrior-sage, the fight is not just a means to an end. The fight is a way of being in the world, an ongoing labour of love.'[1]

In 1793, Sahib Kaur was, at the age of 18, the first Sikh woman to become Prime Minister of Patiali. This warrior and leader of men, who played a prominent part in the history of the Sutlej states from 1793 to 1801, was the elder sister of Raja Sahib Singh of Patiala. This was the first time, globally, that a woman became the political leader of a region.

Princess Sophia Jindan Alexandra Duleep Singh was the daughter of Maharaja Duleep Singh, the last Maharaja of the Sikh Empire. He was known as the Black Prince of Perthshire and was the first Sikh to settle in Scotland. Sophia made a trip to India with her sisters, in 1903, that altered her world view dramatically, transforming her from socialite to royal revolutionary. The Indian officials she met held little regard for her. She encountered racism and witnessed the abject poverty and famine endured by people living under British rule.

On her return to London, Sophia became involved in the movement for Women's Suffrage, joined the Women's Tax Resistance League

---

1   Valarie Kaur, *See No Stranger,* 2020

and the Suffragette Fellowship, and became an active member of the Women's Social and Political Union. Sophia joined many other women, including Mrs. Emmeline Pankhurst, in campaigning for a change in the law, which at that time denied women the right to vote. On February 6, 1918, the Representation of the People Act was passed, giving the vote to women aged over 30 who met property qualifications. In 1919, the first female MP, Nancy Astor, entered the Commons and finally, in 1928, the British parliament passed the Representation of the People Act, which meant that women were granted the right to vote on the same terms as men, though women had to be over 30 years old, compared to the age limit for men of 21 years old. In 2018, Sophia was honoured by the Royal Mail with a stamp marking the centenary of this Act. Princess Sophia Duleep Singh represents a wonderful role model for all Sikh women.

The warrior tradition of Sikhs is exemplified by the battle of Saragarhi, described beautifully in Jay Singh Sohal's book, *Saragarhi – Forgotten Battle*. I met Jay in March 2013 when he brought his Turbanology Exhibition to the Edinburgh City Chambers. Sikh Sanjog, Edinburgh Lothian Racial Equality Council and Edinburgh Interfaith Association had worked in partnership with other organisations to bring this exhibition to Scotland. It was a huge success with over one hundred people attending and learning about the history of the turban or Dastar, as it is sometimes called.

Saragarhi tells the story of a battle between Afghan insurgents and the 36th Sikh Regiment. Jay was launching the book at Sandhurst and had sent me an invitation, so I took along my son, Rajvinder, and grandson, Jeevan. Sandhurst is steeped in history that I found enthralling, I couldn't get enough of its paintings, artefacts and architecture. It's an establishment that only the elite of English aristocracy – and a privileged few from the Sikh community – have experienced. But I wished there and then that I was 40 years younger.

I would have joined up like a shot! It was such an extraordinary day and we were in awe of our surroundings.

Sandhurst was a place that I had heard of but I was completely unaware of how it could possibly have any links with Sikhs. There is even a room with a stained glass window that has the Sikh soldiers depicted in battle.

Jay's book recounts the epic battle of 1897 between 21 men of the 36th Sikh Regiment (currently the 4th Sikh Regiment) and Afghan insurgents. These Sikhs were fighting for a queen and country they had never seen, yet they were willing to give up their lives in the line of duty. They fought to the death rather than surrender.

The Battle at Saragarhi is one of eight stories of collective bravery published by UNESCO. It has been mentioned as one of the five most significant events of its kind in the world, and these include the Saga of Thermopylae, the heroic stand of a small Greek force against the mighty Persian Army of Xerxes in 480 B.C.

The defenders of Saragarhi, under the indomitable and inspiring leadership of their detachment commander, Havildar Ishar Singh, resolved to defend their post and fight to the last, in the best tradition of their race and regiment. They were not prepared to hand over the post to the enemy and seek safety elsewhere, despite knowing full well that a handful of men in a makeshift fort of stones and mud walls with a wooden door could not possibly stand against the onslaught of thousands of tribesmen.

The Indian Government erected a stone tablet to the memory of the 21 non-commissioned officers and men of the 36th Sikh Regiment of the Bengal Infantry, whose names are engraved on it as a perpetual record of the heroism shown by these gallant soldiers. They died at their posts in the defence of the fort of Saragarhi, on the 12th of September 1897, fighting against overwhelming numbers, thus proving their loyalty and devotion to their sovereign, the Queen

Empress of India, and gloriously maintaining the reputation of the Sikhs for unflinching courage on the field of battle.

This episode, when narrated in the British Parliament at that time, drew from the members a standing ovation in the memory of the defenders of Saragarhi. The story of the heroic deeds of these men was also placed before Queen Victoria. The account was received all over the world with awe and admiration. All 21 valiant men of this epic battle were posthumously awarded the Indian Order of Merit Class III, which at the time was one of the highest gallantry awards given to Indian troops, and is considered equivalent to the present-day *Vir Chakra*. All dependants of the Saragarhi heroes were awarded 50 acres of land and 500 rupees. Never before or since has a complete body of men each won a gallantry award in a single action. It is, indeed, a singularly unique event in the annals of Indian military history.

FAMILY

The most important element in the Sikh community, anywhere in the world, is the family.

'Family' means the extended family. The young child's first loyalty is to their family, especially the link with their mother, and to the extended family and the Sikh community, locally and universally, the Khalsa Panth.

The first fundamental influences on the character of the Sikh child are not from the 'outside' western culture – they are the influences of home – mother, father, sisters and brothers. The ideal personality that the Sikh parents try to form in their children is conformist, loyal, and co-operative, moderate in their demands and expectations, and self-discipline.

The accepted beliefs and moral standards of the family and

the community are taken for granted and they are not subjects for questioning or discussion. However, with changing times, communities have adapted and evolved as we move into fourth and fifth generations of Sikhs being born in the U.K. We can no longer hold onto the cultural values that were embedded in us over 60 years ago.

Everything in the Sikh child's early life encourages that child to expect and to want the emotional security that only the family can give. The family itself is subject to the scrutiny of the wider group, the Sikh community in the neighbourhood, and its branches elsewhere. The individual who accepts the protection and stability of the family is obliged to protect its good name by living up to the standard of the community.

In conforming to traditions, the home upbringing of Bhat Sikh girls was largely preparation for marriage and motherhood. They were not encouraged to take up employment, although attitudes have changed dramatically over the past 20 years. The Bhat Sikh communities in England tend to be more progressive in their attitudes than the Scottish Bhat community which myself and my family live in.

Sikhs usually lived in extended and joint families, under one roof, with parents and grandparents taking care of their children and grandchildren. The seniors or grandparents had a great role to play – they were the head of the families. They had experience of life, having already gone through its ups and downs.

Nowadays, new values are being determined by the generations of Sikhs who are now dual culture citizens and the nuclear family concept has taken over in many families. Sometimes, we have to acknowledge that, painful as it is, we are not immune to a changing world. Sadly, life is not very kind to senior citizens in foreign countries due to role reversals. In the traditional family hierarchy, the parents are recognised as head of the family. This role of authority and respect diminishes and reverses when the parents immigrate to foreign countries. Their children make all the decisions regarding properties, household and financial affairs.

This has led to a breakdown of the extended family as we once knew it within many Sikh communities, across the board. It is becoming something that all Sikhs from all walks of life have to address in whatever way is best suited to their needs and their family. This topic is not discussed openly as people feel that to talk to others about the changes taking place within their family structure will affect the family pride and honour, and this is always foremost before personal health, happiness and well-being. They believe that such information may bring shame and humiliation to the name of their family.

DRESS: MEN AND TURBANS

The way Sikhs dress is due to their culture and is very different from any other religious group. Men can be identified by the turban, which is normally made from muslin and is five metres long. The turban must always be worn by a Sikh man when he is in public and also at mealtimes, but he may take it off in the privacy of his own home and when he goes to bed. The Sikh man wears the turban to keep his uncut hair (Kesh), tidy and clean. However, unlike the women, most men wear western-style clothes in Britain, apart from a turban. Some Sikh men do have their hair cut and are called Sehjdhari.

Guru Gobind Singh, the tenth and last Guru, created the Khalsa. In Punjabi this means 'the Pure' – the purified and reconstituted Sikh community instituted by Guru Gobind Singh on March 30, 1699 – Baisakhi Day or Vaisakhi (as it is also known). Khalsa Sikhs celebrate the birth of the order on April 13th of each year. Boys are presented with the turban in a special ceremony at the Gurdwara from the age of five upwards, but this is a choice for the family. Before this time, they wear their hair in a 'jura' (top knot) or wear a 'Patka' (bandana).

DRESS: WOMEN

Many Sikh women wear shalwar-kameez, which is a long tunic and matching trousers. The reason why most Sikh women wear shalwar-kameez is that they cover their bodies respectfully and modestly from head to toe whilst in public. This form of dress is both very comfortable and practical to wear because of its looseness. It allows for a lot of movement, which is especially needed when praying or entering the temple and sitting on the floor. Some women wear another form of dress, the sari. This originally came from India, whereas the shalwar-kameez came from the Punjab area, from where most Sikhs originated. The sari is six metres in length. However, in adapting to life in the UK, most young Sikh women now wear full western dress at all times, except when attending weddings, parties and festivals.

We are slowly letting our culture slip away, not from choice but out of necessity. It is more practical to wear western clothes, but Sikh women also feel less conspicuous at a time when hostility toward people of colour is not uncommon. New cultural values are being determined by our lifestyle and where we live and, painful though it is to have to acknowledge that we are not immune to the need to make changes, these adaptations are vital to the continued well-being of Sikhs, both as individuals and as communities. There is now an increase in young Sikh women also wearing the Turban/Dastar as there is an increase in Sikh religious awareness amongst the younger generations.

Veils

In Indian family life, purdah (from the Hindi *parda*, literally, curtain), or the veiling and seclusion of women, is a tradition in much of northern and central India, particularly in rural areas. Both Hindu and Muslim women follow complex rules of veiling the body and avoidance of public appearance, especially in the presence of relatives linked by marriage and before strange men. Purdah practices are inextricably linked to patterns of authority and harmony within the family. Rules of Hindu and Muslim purdah differ in certain key ways, but female modesty and decorum, as well as concepts of family honour, are essential to the various forms of purdah. In most areas, purdah restrictions were stronger for women of high-status families.

Such rules of feminine modesty are not considered purdah but merely proper female behaviour. For traditional Hindus of northern and central India, purdah observances begin at marriage, when a woman acquires a husband and in-laws. Although she almost never observes purdah in her natal home or before her natal relatives, a woman did observe purdah in her husband's home and before his relatives.

How did the custom of veiling come to India and infiltrate our communities and become our culture?[2] Women in India have always been accorded pride of place in both religious and philosophical thought. They were capable of advanced learning in every branch of knowledge and enjoyed high status in society in Vedic times. Historically, head coverings can be found in many cultures throughout the world, including the West. The first records we have of women who wore head coverings are from Assyria in the 13th century, BC. These first instances of head coverings were markers of

---

2   Pran Nevile, Beyond the Veil: Indian Women in the Raj, 2000

social standing. Women of nobility began wearing head coverings in order to differentiate themselves from women of lower social status. Throughout history, head coverings have been worn for various reasons. These include being markers of class or religious beliefs, as well as for practical uses, as social practices, as fashion trends and as traditional dress.

However, the wearing of veils was outlawed within the Sikh scriptures by Guru Amar Das, the 4th Guru, in the 15th century. Amar Das considered that the wearing of veils by women was demeaning and he implemented the hukam (law) that no woman should enter the Gurdwara wearing a veil over her face. Guru Ji refused an audience with a Hindu queen until she had removed her veil.

Personally, I was always confused about the whole business of veiling. As we grew older and the community became more mixed, we would see other Sikh women going about without covering their heads or, more remarkably to me, hiding their faces with the veil from anyone. This confused me and, when I would question this, I was told that our Bhat community held the practice of veiling in great esteem as it showed respect for elders.

Yet it seemed to me that Sikh women living in Great Britain in the 20th century were being subjected to this oppression, a tyranny that we couldn't challenge because we were invariably invisible. I even have a photo of me, holding my baby, veiled, because it was taken at a festival and my husband's eldest brother was taking the picture! I stopped observing this custom in the late 80s. Some women from our community had stopped veiling but they were few and far between and were always open to abuse from other women who deemed them to have become open and shameless. Thankfully, this custom is now almost extinct, even in the Bhat community.

SIKH FESTIVALS

A Sikh festival or holy day is called a Gurpurab, meaning Guru's Remembrance Day. The celebration is generally similar for all Gurpurabs, only the hymns and history of a particular occasion are different.

BAISAKHI

Also called **Vaisakhi,** Baisakhi is the birthday of the Khalsa (the Pure Ones), and is generally celebrated on the 13th of April every year.

The Khalsa was formed by Guru Gobind Singh at Vaisakhi in AD 1699. It is a group into which committed Sikhs can be initiated to demonstrate their devotion to their faith.

The Khalsa commemorates five volunteers who were prepared to offer their lives for Waheguru and Guru Gobind Singh. Their commitment is an example of sewa – a willingness to serve others without thought for your own wellbeing.

After offering their lives to Guru Gobind Singh, the five volunteers were given amrit, which is a mixture of sugar and water. They were given it in a bowl stirred by a khanda – a double-edged sword. This represented them being initiated into the Khalsa. Guru Gobind Singh then declared them the first five members of the Khalsa. They became known as the Panj Pyare – the five beloved ones.

Guru Gobind Singh and his wife were then initiated into the Khalsa. Guru Gobind Singh declared that all men who were initiated into the Khalsa would be given the name 'Singh', meaning 'lion', and all women who were initiated would be given the name 'Kaur', meaning 'princess'. This indicates the removal of status or caste and represents equality and fairness within all humaniy.

AMRIT

This ceremony is held and given to those who offer themselves for Sikh initiation. This service can be held at any time of the year. Sikhs who have taken Amrit are called Khalsa.

DIWALI

The Diwali ceremony celebrates the return of the sixth Guru to Amritsar in 1620, after his release from Gwalior Jail. (Emperor Jahangir had imprisoned him because he was afraid of the Guru's growing power and popularity with the masses). Diwali, which means festival of lights, is celebrated by both Sikhs and Hindus, and generally falls in November. It takes the form of a one-day celebration held both in the Gurdwara and in homes and businesses. These places are illuminated at night with divas (oil lamps made of clay), candles or fireworks.

At home my mum would place 25 candles in a tray and have trays of fruit and sweets and all our money, wallets, jewellery would be placed alongside this to be blessed. A small bowl with saffron would be put on our foreheads (like a tilak) as we bowed our heads in reverence to the candles and also our ancestors. We would then take the burning candles and place them in plates and put them in every room in the house, bringing light and prosperity to each space for the next year!

Again, in the Bhat community, there was the added ritual of, on the second day of Diwali, in the morning, my mother making 25 small chapattis from plain flour, heated on the griddle with oil. She would spread newspaper on the floor then set out the tray with the chapattis and a pot of prashadh (fresh butter and sugar in semolina) on the paper, together with a jug of water. The whole family would then sit down on the floor. Mum would hold five chappatis in her hand at a time, break off bits and dip them in the prashadh, meanwhile murmuring names under her breath. The prashadh-dipped chapatti pieces were placed on a plate. This ritual continued until all 25 chapattis had been so treated. Mum would then take the jug and pour water right round the tray (hence the newspaper) so it would not mess up the carpet! Then the rest of the family had to wait whilst we three sisters ate what we wanted from the plate before they could get any!

LOHRI

Celebrated primarily by Sikhs, Hindus and Jains, this festival is celebrated every year on January 13 with much enthusiasm and zeal. According to the Indian calendar, Lohri falls in the month of Pausha and is followed by the festival of kites, Makar Sankranti. The origin of the festival can be traced back to the legend of Dulla Bhatti: it is believed that Dulla Bhatti was a robber, but he rescued and saved many girls from slave markets. So, the people sing songs to express their gratitude towards him. He is widely described in the folklore of Punjab.

The festival of Lohri holds great significance as it marks the harvest of the rabi crops and the end of winter days. The day is observed by all communities with different names. People sing and dance around the Lohri fire and throw foods like gajak, popcorn, puffed rice and others into the fire as 'tributes' to the gods in exchange for blessings. The gathering would then go from house to house singing songs of joy and asking that any parents of boys welcome them with gifts of money, popcorn or sweets.

Lohri is considered especially auspicious for newlywed couples and parents with newborn babies because it marks fertility. The festival also holds great importance for farmers.

The Bhat community celebrated it in their own way and as people were now living in Great Britain, they had to adapt the festival to suit their new way of life. Living in tenements with no yards to light fires, they made mountains of popcorn and piled it onto a bed or the floor. It was especially marked by the birth of a baby boy. The baby boy is held by individual members of family and friends and bounced up and down in the popcorn.

Back in the 50s and 60s, even up to the 70s, popcorn was thrown onto the fire burning in the fireplace while traditional songs were sung by the older women. Nowadays people use barbeques or even have bonfires in their back gardens but sadly, some of the more traditional songs which were particular to the Bhat community are being lost as more and more young people have stopped celebrating this festival. There has been a revival in India so hopefully we may still see it happening in the UK in the future. One aspect that has changed in the younger generation here, and in India, is that now this festival celebrates births of both boys and girls, even within the Bhat community.

THUMDEY

is performed in June, is unique to Bhat Sikhs and is celebrated at home. The festival assumes even greater importance if the family have recently bought a new house, been blessed by the birth of a baby boy, or enjoyed an engagement or wedding. The rituals of this festival include the purchase of five jugs or kettles and new clothes, which are given to the girls of the family; money is also given. Like the ritual on the second day of Diwali, my mother would make small chapattis from plain flour, heated on the griddle with oil: she made 52 if there had been a major event such as the birth of a son or the purchase of a house, otherwise the number was 25.

One such day, I asked my mum what she murmured under her breath during this ritual and she said that we were remembering our ancestors in the act of breaking the chappatis and mixing them with the prashadh. I was horrified. I said that meant we girls were eating food dedicated to dead people, how could they get any if we ate it first? My mum told me not to be silly, that it was a ritual that had been observed for years. I then asked her about the water that she poured around the tray which held the 'holy food' dedicated to dead people. The answer was the same, that it symbolised the giving of water to our ancestors before we ate the food. So, I persisted, how does the water and the food reach these dead people? I was told to be quiet and just eat.

Little did I know that 15 years on, as a married woman, I too would be performing the same rituals, for at least another 15 years. I then came to the realisation that I had to stop as there was no religious connection to any of this ritual. When I was questioned by my children about this ritual and festival, I did not have a rational answer for them. And, indeed, this festival is now slowly dying out in Bhat communities as more and more people realise that Thumdey is a ritual without any religious foundation that has existed simply because it was performed by one's parents and must be passed onto one's children.

LAKRIYA, ALSO KNOWN AS RAKHI OR RAKHSHA BANDAN

this festival is celebrated in August and, like Diwali, is observed by both Hindus and Sikhs. It is a celebration of the love between brothers and sisters. The sisters make food at home and put sweetmeats onto a tray. The ritual with regards to food is different within the Bhat community, compared with other sects.

45

About a week before Lakhriya, my mum would make a soft dough from white plain flour, then powder a large silver tray lightly with plain flour. She would then sit for hours rolling a small amount of dough between her finger and thumb to make small pieces of vermicelli, which would be laid out in 3 or 4 trays and allowed to dry for a week. On the morning of Lakhriya, she put the pieces into a pot of boiling water for 10 to 15 minutes, drained them, then mixed them with butter and sugar boiled together and guess what? We girls ate them first!

Sisters also buy brightly coloured threads and entwine them together (similar to friendship bracelets). The Rakhi thread is tied onto the brother's wrist, then he is given a piece of sweetmeat. He, in turn, will give his sister money. Historically, in times of war, Hindu girls were frequently kidnapped by Muslims. If they were rescued by Sikhs, the girls would be encouraged to tie Rakhi threads to their rescuers' wrists, signifying they were safe in their company because they had become their brothers for life.

We couldn't buy our Rakhis, back in the 1950s and 60s, so we would sit with wool, embroidery thread and beads and make them by hand. Today, everything can be bought on Amazon or Raksha Bandhan websites, but I think we had the best fun making them by hand, competing to see who made the best ones.

KURVA CHAUTH VURTH (FAST)

This festival is celebrated in October by both Hindu and Sikh women; it signifies the love for a husband by his wife. The day starts at about 4 a.m. when the women rise, wash and pray and eat special food, namely yoghurt, fruit and special chapattis. They fast for the rest of the day. At around mid-afternoon they bathe then dress in red, as this is the traditional colour for a bride, and adorn themselves with jewellery. A tray is prepared with sugar, milk, butter and fruit (coconut, melon or pomegranate). They then wait until the full moon rises and only then do they break their fast.

In truth, this festival should not be practised by Sikh women because fasting is against Sikh principles. The rituals practised derive from ancestral traditions and older women, especially in the Bhat community, are ambivalent about doing away with it. This is because superstition still plays a major role in their lives. They feel this festival must continue as it ensures their husbands are blessed with a long life by the gods.

I also celebrated this festival with great enthusiasm in the early days of my marriage. It was very romantic! My husband would bring me all sorts of sweets and chocolates as we waited for the moon to show itself. His mother would read the story of the woman who sacrificed her life out of love for her husband and we all had to sit and listen to this before we broke the fast.

There was lots of fun in the early days of our marriage, as our husbands and brothers-in-law would tease us by saying, 'It's there, the moon's out,' and we would all run out into the street only to find big black clouds floating around. The funniest time was when my husband's granny, Inder Kaur, moved above us into a tenement block. If the weather was bad, we would crouch on the landing stairwell with the window open and throw our sacrifices of milk to the moon through the window. We always wondered what passers-by must have thought if they got caught by a spray of milk from above!

My take on Vurth was always at odds with my female relations. As I came to understand more about the Sikh religion, I began to realise that these rituals held no real meaning and were, in fact, quite detrimental. They created fear within women that, if they stopped practising or adhering to these rituals, then bad omens would befall their husbands. I stopped practising Vurth in 2003 – with my

47

husband's blessings, I may say!

AKHAND PATH

In 1742, when Sikhs lived in the jungles of Punjab, one Sikh woman warrior named Bibi Sundari requested, just before she died due to wounds suffered in battle, to have an Akhand Path arranged for her. She lay there next to the Guru Granth Sahib and listened to the full recitation of this Path. After kirtan, Ardas and Hukam, she received the Karah Prashad, then uttered 'Waheguru ji ka Khalsa, Waheguru ji Ki Fateh' as she breathed her last. Thus began the tradition of reading an Akhand Path in 48 hours.

The continuous recitation (without any break) of the Guru Granth Sahib[3] from beginning to end, (all 1430 pages), is made by a team of readers and lasts about 48 hours. This ritual is considered a very holy practice and is said to bring peace and solace both to the participants and to listeners of the recitation. During the reading, it is traditional to make langar (communal food) available at all times, thus requiring the continual service and dedication of those in whose honour the Akhand Path is being held.

The recitation (or Path) is undertaken for various reasons. It can be to mark a happy or sad occasion within the family, or simply to increase one's feeling of connection to Waheguru. Some may call for an Akhand Path depending on events within a family such as a birth, birthday, recovery from a medical operation, wedding, death,

---

3 Literally, 'the first book'; the name given to the collection of hymns compiled by Guru Arjan Dev Ji, the fifth Guru, in 1604, which formed the basis of the Holy Sikh Scriptures.

graduation, an achievement (such as a high school certificate or passing a driving test), an anniversary, historic occasion and so on.

Some Gurdwaras hold a weekly Akhand Path which gives the congregation (Sadh_Sangat) an opportunity to establish a close relationship with the Guru and the community. It also provides an opportunity to carry out volunteer work (Seva), thus obtaining the blessing of the Guru's Word to the whole of the community.

THE CELEBRATION OF GURU NANAK'S BIRTHDAY AND OF OTHER GURUS

The birthday of Guru Nanak, founder of the Sikh religion, usually comes in the month of November, but the date varies from year to year, based on the traditional dates of the Indian calendar. The celebration usually lasts three days. An Akhand Path is held in the Gurdwara two days before the birthday, followed the next day by a procession led by the Panj Pyaras (Five Beloved Ones) and the Palki (Palanquin) of Siri Guru Granth Sahib.

The procession is followed by teams of singers singing hymns, brass bands, 'Gatka' (martial art teams) showing their swordsmanship and devotees singing Shabdhs (hymns). The procession passes through streets covered with bunting, and decorated gates, while the leaders inform the people of the message of Guru Nanak. On the actual birthday, the programme begins at about 4 or 5 a.m., with the singing of Asa-di-Var (morning hymns) and hymns from the Sikh scriptures. This is followed by Katha (exposition of the scripture) and lectures and recitation of poems in praise of the Guru. The celebrations continue until 1 to 2 p.m.

After Ardas and the distribution of Karah Parshad (a sweet pudding made of equal parts of flour, sugar and ghee or clarified butter, and three parts water) at the end of the service, the Langar is served.

Some Gurdwara also hold a night session which begins at sunset, when Rehras (evening prayer) is recited. This is followed by Kirtan till late in the night. Sometimes a Kavi-darbar (poetic symposium) is also held to enable poets to pay their tributes to the Guru in their own verses. At about 1.20 a.m., the actual time of the Guru's birth, the congregation sings praises of the Guru and recites the Holy Word. The function ends about 2 a.m.

Sikhs who cannot join the celebrations for some reason, or who do not have access to a Sikh temple, hold the ceremony in their own homes by performing Kirtan, Path, Ardas, Karah Parshad and Langar.

GURU GOBIND SINGH

The birthday of Guru Gobind Singh, the tenth Guru, generally falls in December or January. The celebrations are similar to those of Guru Nanak's birthday, namely Akhand Path, procession and Kirtan, Katha, and Langar.

GURU ARJAN

The anniversary of the martyrdom of Guru Arjan, the fifth Guru, falls in May or June, the hottest months in India. He was tortured to death under the orders of the Moghul Emperor, Jahangir, at Lahore on 25th May 1606. Celebrations consist of Kirtan, Katha, lectures, Karah Parshad and Langar in the Gurdwara. Because this ceremony is held in summer, a chilled sweetened drink made from milk, sugar and water is freely distributed in Gurdwaras and in neighbourhoods to everybody, irrespective of their religious belief.

Guru Tegh Bahadur

The ninth Guru, was arrested under orders of the Moghul Emperor, Aurangzeb. As he refused to change his religion and accept Islam, he was beheaded on 11th November 1675 at Chandi Chowk, Delhi.

Guru Gobind Singh

Three days before his passing away, Guru Gobind Singh conferred, on the 3rd October 1708, perpetual Gurudom on Siri Guru Granth Sahib. On this day, a special one-day celebration is held with Kirtan, Katha, lectures, Ardas, Karah Parshad and Langar. Sikhs rededicate themselves to following the teachings of the Gurus contained in the scriptures at this ceremony.

The different Sikh Communities (Sects) and their establishment in the United Kingdom

The Bhat or Bhattra community, also known as the Sangat Bhat or the Bhat Sikh community, are a group of Sikhs whose origins lie in the Punjab. Bhat tradition and traditional Sikh literature say their ancestors came from Sri Lanka and were the original 16th century followers of Guru Nanak, the founder of Sikhism. In the 17th century, some religious Bhat went to fight as 'warrior-saints' against Mughal persecution in the Khalsa campaign, inspired by Guru Gobind Singh Ji. Since many Bhat lived as travelling missionaries, their mobility led them to depend on occupations that did not require a settled life. By the 19th century, Bhat was the name of a caste or jati within the Indian tradition of social classes, each with its own occupation.

There are many Sikh communities, or sects, within the

51

UK, including, most notably, Jats, Ramgharia and Bhat. These communities differ in many ways in the way they conduct their daily lives, but the religious side of all these communities remains the same. Sikhism recognises no caste or sub-group(s). Some communities have remained traditional in their ways and still practice rituals and customs that have been discarded by other Sikh communities.

In India, the Bhat community was mainly concentrated in the districts of Lahore and Gujranwala, and the surrounding villages of Bhadewala and Galotiakalan, now in Pakistan. They moved to India in 1947 after the partition. Their traditional occupation is handreading. There has long been a tradition of overseas migration among the Bhat Sikhs. Migration of Bhat Sikhs to Britain began in the 1920s[4] and they earned their living by hawking suitcases of clothing from door to door. They have been praised for their business acumen, described as people with 'a spirit of enterprise'.

In the 1920s, some men travelled to Britain to work as door-to-door salesmen, most leaving their families in the Punjab to begin with. By the time of the Second World War, there were a few hundred Sikhs clustered in British seaports like Cardiff, Bristol and Southampton. Some British Bhat communities still have links to one or two particular villages.

Today, in the United Kingdom, there are significant numbers of Sikhs with Bhat ancestry, as there are in India. In the Punjab, most Bhat Sikhs are now in Patiala, Amritsar, Hoshiarpur, Gurdaspur or Bhathinda districts, or in Jullunder or Chandigarh; elsewhere in India, they tend to live in cities, particularly Delhi and Calcutta. Although Bhat Sikhs started to arrive in the United Kingdom in the 1920s, most came in the late 1940s or 1950s. Even though Sikhism itself does not support separation by caste, the social system meant that the Bhat followed a hereditary profession of itinerant salesman,

4   (Ballard and Ballard, 1977:28; Nesbitt 1980:56)

while some also foretold the future if they were considered to have clairvoyant ability. Interaction between Bhats and other Sikh groups in the past was very minimal. Apart from meeting at the gurdwara, it was virtually non-existent. In the past, most other sects of Sikhs regarded Bhat as a low caste group but admired their commitment to the Sikh tradition.

Sikhs have had a presence in the UK for over 160 years and, during that time, they have become well-integrated within British society. The first Sikh known to have settled here was Maharaja Duleep Singh in 1854. There has been steady migration from India to Britain since then. Even before the First World War, a few hardy individuals came to Britain to peddle clothes and ribbons in the villages. But the influx of Sikh migrants into the UK increased enormously in the chaotic aftermath of the 1947 division of 'British' India into the secular, but largely Hindu state of India, and the Muslim state of Pakistan. The arbitrary partition of the Punjab, in which one part was ceded to Pakistan and the other part to India, gave the Bhat Sikh Community a greater reason to migrate to Britain. Many had already visited the UK before that time and had relations firmly established there. The Bhat Sikhs were the pioneer Sikh community in these migrations to Britain. Whilst most men from other Sikh communities were just establishing a foothold in Britain in the late 1940s and early 1950s, the Bhats had already formed settled communities all over Britain, particularly in ports and cities.

Each wave of Sikh migrants to the UK brought with it its own cultural beliefs, yet these migrants managed to integrate themselves within British society whilst retaining their distinct identity. According to the 2011 Census, there are approximately 430,000 Sikhs throughout the UK, while the number in Scotland is approximately 10,000.

The Sikh Community in Glasgow and Edinburgh

The Sikh community in Glasgow was established around the late 40s, early 50s with Sikh families living in the Gorbals, Kelvinside and Maryhill. In fact, there were pockets of Sikhs across Glasgow, sometimes unaware of each other. The first Gurdwara in Glasgow was established around 1957/8 in South Portland Street in the Gorbals. Then around 1963/4, as the community began to expand, there was movement of large swathes of the community leaving the Gorbals and moving to Pollokshields. The Gurdwara in South Portland Street was sold and bigger premises were purchased in 163 Nithsdale Road.

However, as my story is about my life in Edinburgh, I will focus on the development of the Sikh community in Edinburgh. It began in 1958 and comprised small family groups that originated from the same area in the Punjab. They initially came to London, and from there travelled to various parts of Scotland, plying their trades of door-to-door selling, palmistry and fortune-telling. Their settlement in Edinburgh was in a small area of Leith, specifically Hamilton Street, Wilkie Place, Springfield Street and St Mary's Street. The first Gurdwara in Edinburgh was established in 1964 at 7 Hope Terrace, Leith. The Gurdwara was moved in 1970, to 11 Academy Street, Leith, to accommodate the growing community. In 1976 the Gurdwara was moved again to its current location at 1 Sheriff Brae, Leith. The building, previously St Thomas' Church, was constructed in 1843. Over the past 50 years, the Bhat community has grown to a population of over 2000+, due both to an influx from England and Ireland, and to a steady trickle of students and their families from India.

3

My Marriage

In early 1973, when I was 19 years old, my big sister was told by her mother-in-law to speak to my parents and ask if they would consider me being engaged to Johnny, her brother-in-law. He had been engaged to a girl in Middlesborough for the past few years but this had not worked out and the engagement had been broken off; would my parents consider me being engaged to him? My parents were hesitant at first and I can't quite remember how my sister told me, but I was told to pretend I didn't know anything about it.

I was a bit shocked to begin with because, even though we used to visit my sister a lot and Johnny used to come to Glasgow with her, I had never given him a second look or thought. My head was always filled with film stars and fantasies. But then my sister showed me a photo of him. He had just had his hair cut and I think I fell in love with him right there and then. But it wasn't a straightforward engagement because, when the people in Middlesborough heard that Johnny was going to be engaged to his sister-in-law's sister, they started to spread rumours that my sister had been the one behind the break-up so she could then bring her sister into the family. I was to find out later that my husband had actually said to his mother that if he was to get married to an Indian girl, it had to be Trishna, otherwise it wasn't going to happen.

In those days, for a man to make such a statement was unheard of. My mother-in-law would tell me the story, as did my husband many times, of the time he was standing at the bus stop in Leith Walk, outside Millers Carpet shop, and his mother was getting on at him.

As his first engagement had broken down, she was worried that this would affect the prospects of his siblings getting married. He needed to decide what he would do and agree to her looking for a girl for him. It was then that he said to her that he wanted to marry me, Trishna. She was totally taken aback and started questioning him about how and why had he decided this? He told her that he had seen me many times when he visited our house with my sister, and he thought I was the person for him.

Indian engagements and weddings in those days were very complicated, drawn-out processes. In their hearts and minds, our parents were still living in their villages in India, so the wedding rituals had to follow the old traditional patterns. Looking back on it now, this protracted process was rather wonderful and romantic; it created many memories in a way that perhaps doesn't occur in Indian weddings now.

My parents wanted to wait until all these malicious rumours had died down before they did anything publicly. But word spread very quickly, and a couple of weeks later, when I went to the Gurdwara, my friends, Amrita and Santosh, (who lived in Nithsdale Road) had heard of this 'engagement'. They approached me and said, 'Hey, we've seen your future hubby, he's gorgeous and looks like Rajesh Khanna, the actor.' I was really amazed that they knew and I had to pretend that it was news to me. When I went home, I said to my sister-in-law, 'Look, this is what they said to me, is it true?' So she told my mum, who actually believed that I really did not know what was happening, even though they were discussing this all around me – unbelievable! So my mum told my sister-in-law to tell me, 'Yes, it was true, it was going to happen,' and I wasn't to phone my sister or write to her.

ENGAGEMENT

In those days, in the 70s in the UK, the ceremonies around engagements and weddings were conducted as they had been in the villages, and these occasions were more about the families coming together. My husband-to-be didn't put a ring on my finger. Rather, his family came through from Edinburgh and the ritual was that they brought with them 25 boxes of fruit and some sweetmeats and a case of sugar. The welcome engagement ceremony was opened by my sister-in-law (who was veiled as there were men older than her husband present) by pouring oil at each side of our doorway. It was important that she did this first on the right side, *then* on the left. Then my sister, Sukhwant, and her husband, Baldev, entered as they were the go-betweens, then came the remainder of the guests, including my husband-to-be's mother, grandmother, aunts and uncles.

The ritual continued with ceremony and prayer and Ardass by the gianni (priest). My family had prepared a large silver tray on which was a block of gur, a gold ring and five chuaray (dried palm dates), all covered by a large scarf. Jaggery, or gur, is a specific type of sugar popular in India. It is normally manufactured from either sugar cane or date palms. Sugar cane jaggery is considered sacred and is consumed before the commencement of a new venture, journey, or business endeavour. The tray was handed over to the 'go-betweens', then my father gave a speech in which he said that he was entrusting the family of the groom with his daughter and that he hoped they would respect and honour her and her family.

After these rituals, we all sat down to a meal – in our house, a flat in a tenement building on the third floor. Altogether, there were at least 50 adults and children as well. The men ate in one room and the women in the other. In those days people didn't hire halls or caterers, everything was done in one's house, the food being cooked and served by the women.

The day culminated with my family giving 25 cases of fruit and sugar plus the tray with the ring, etc. and a tray with 51 laddus, to my husband's family. Laddus, a quintessential Indian sweet savoured on every festival or occasion, are made of flour, fat (ghee-butter oil) and sugar with other ingredients such as chopped nuts or dried raisins that vary by recipe. Across India, the laddu was, and still is, an integral part of wedding and engagement ceremonies. Boxes of laddus get exchanged as soon as an engagement is announced, wedding invitations often come with a box of laddus and laddus are served as a part of the wedding feast. Nowadays, people can buy these sweets in shops but back in the 70s, they were all homemade. A woman who lived in our street in Pollokshields made laddus in her house and people would order boxes from her. She sometimes added fine slivers of silver foil to the laddu for special occasions.

While the rituals were going on, I was upstairs in my bedroom – and my fiancé was back in Edinburgh, waiting for his family to return. Once they had left our house, I was allowed to go downstairs and eat, but I was *not* allowed to show any emotion other than a 'sadness' that this was the first step of my new journey into a new family, with responsibilities of keeping the honour of both families. This was especially so since both my sisters were married and had proven themselves to be good daughters-in-law, gaining respect from all sides of each family. Actually, I was really happy and had to hide this emotion, which was quite weird when I think about it, but that was the way it was.

My mother sat me down and explained how my relationship with my elder sister and brother-in-law would now be different. I could no longer phone or even write to my sister, a real wrench for me because my writing letters to both my sisters had become something of a fixture. I regularly wrote to them about all that was going on and what they were missing in Glasgow. Furthermore, if any of the family came to visit, I was to discreetly remove myself from their company.

This changed my relationships with all sorts of people. For example, my brother-in-law, 'JeeJa Ji' (I had called him that for eight years), had been the butt of many pranks played by me. Once, I blew an egg out using a darning needle (I saw this done on Blue Peter), then placed the empty egg in an eggcup, alongside toast, etc. and presented this Scottish brekkie to my Jeeja. The look on his face when he tapped the egg with his spoon only to reveal an empty shell: hilarious! This was typical of the JeeJa-Trishna relationship. But now I wasn't to talk to him at all until after the wedding.

As the elder brother in his family, when his (and Johnny's) father, Tunda Singh, died in a tragic car accident in 1964, he assumed the role of father figurehead. I was instructed to treat him as my future father-in law and also, after the wedding, I was no longer to address him as JeeJa Ji but 'Bhaiya Ji', meaning respected elder brother; I was also to veil my face in his presence.

I was outraged and upset at all this. Why should it be that I must change my relationship with my brother-in-law so completely? I could, and did, adjust to cutting communications with my sister as she would still be visiting us, so that didn't bother me too much. After the wedding, we could go back to our normal levels of communication. But for my brother-in-law, whom I had known for eight years and with whom I had developed a sisterly relationship, to be now deemed to be my father-in-law, well, the shock and anger were too much. I would never be able to play any pranks on him again!

So I thought about it and then made a decision. I was not going to be told by others what to do all my life. I sat down with my mother and said, 'When I'm in JeeJa's presence, I will cover my face if I have to, but I will not change how I address him.' My mother was horrified, how could I possibly say this? But I was adamant. I said,

'You tell them that I am not going to call him by the formal name. I will address him, as I have done for the past eight years, as "Jeeja Ji".'

And, amazingly, they agreed! So my journey of standing up for myself and my rights as a woman had begun. The wedding date was fixed for the 29th of July 1974. However the beginning of the wedding would start with the Sehj Patt, which is a reading of the Guru Granth Sahib (Sikh Scriptures). This whole ceremony would begin on the 8th of July 1974 and culminate on the 31st of July 1974. Little did I know what lay ahead.

One of the issues I had to contend with was the wearing of veils. I have described the beliefs and traditions behind the wearing of veils by Sikhs and Indians. Now, the custom was about to become up close and personal for me. How could it be that all these women around me covered their faces from people that were family, but then happily went outside for shopping, etc. with their faces uncovered for all and sundry to see? I was truly baffled and had no idea how I was going to survive this dilemma when it came to the crunch. I was just about to find out.

THE PRE-WEDDING DAYS: 27TH AND 28TH JULY

During the four week period leading up to the wedding rituals, I washed my face only with soap and water, kept my hair in a very straight plait and did not wear any fancy clothes. This really didn't bother me much as we had always been brought up to dress simply and had never been allowed to wear our hair in any other fashion than a straight single plait, with the parting in the middle: no curls, side partings or braids, and no makeup.

The wedding days were five days of rituals and customs that were lovely but very taxing, emotionally and physically. Similar rituals were performed for the groom, so two sets of rituals ran in parallel in separate cities, in Scottish tenement buildings. And, in each building, there were at least eight to ten white Scottish families who were totally unaware of what was going on. I didn't have any white Scottish friends to invite as I wasn't allowed to socialise after I left school at age 13.

Day one of the rituals saw me being covered in a paste of oil and turmeric, both morning and evening, whilst the female contingent of my family sang really sad wedding songs. These were all about how I was leaving the nest and flying away like a bird to a new home. The next day was much of the same, with a henna ritual in the evening.

The classic *mehendi* song, *Mehndi Ni Mehndi,* describes the bride-to-be's happiness at putting henna on her hands for her groom. She talks about the design she wants for the *mehendi* and how her entire family have come together to celebrate her happiness. She feels that the henna is enough to decorate her, and her husband will be pleased at seeing the dark henna on her hands that symbolises the love she has for him. This and other songs were sung all night once the henna had been smeared all over the prospective bride's hands and feet with every member of the family taking a turn at daubing. There were no fancy designs or henna specialists on call then. In fact, the henna was supposed to be applied in a straightforward and simple manner, hence the reason why it felt like having a pair of boxing gloves on your hands and boots on your feet once everyone had done their wee bit!

The third day, 28th July, was the eve of the wedding, and again there were two sets of rituals going on in parallel in two different cities. Rituals that, in India, would have been carried out in courtyards were being performed in the Scottish context in hallways or 'lobbies'.

In those days, we didn't have back gardens, just a communal, wee bit of green space for putting out the washing, or nothing. The day started with me getting up with the henna suitably caked and dried onto both hands and feet. My mum then sat down and shook off the dried henna and wrapped it in a scarf. I was instructed to stay put, only to go to the loo and not to look in the mirror. I was not even allowed to use soorma, which is a superfine powder used in India as an eye application since time immemorial.

It is believed that soorma was first developed by ancient healers for keeping eyes healthy and cool. The powder used to be kept in fancy metal bottles with beautiful carved metal screw top lids which had a long, pencil-like end. This was dipped into the bottle then applied to the inside of the lower eyelids. It certainly transformed one's appearance from a plain, simple girl into a dusky-eyed beauty – but it was only to be used *after* marriage. Woe betide the girl who used soorma before marriage, she would be deemed a hussy!

Day three started at about 11 a.m. when I was taken out of my room by my sister-in-law to our hallway landing where a circle, or rangoli, had been created from plain chappati flour. A small stool comprising a decorated piece of wood was placed in the centre of the rangoli, supposedly facing the sun but, remember, we were in the lobby of a tenement house in Glasgow on the third floor. It was difficult to see the sun at all from there. All my female relatives gathered round me, and then I was told to sit on my haunches on the piece of wood whilst they all sang songs and stripped all my clothes off and washed me with a mixture of milk, yogurt and warm water – no soap!

I was dried off and dressed in a traditional Punjabi dress, a beautiful red salwar kameez. Then I was taken into a room where a tray was placed in front of me; this carried a small diva and some jaggery. I was told to keep looking at the light of the diva as it would make me look more beautiful. Then two pieces of finely decorated half coconuts were tied to my steel bangles ('kara', that even after 47 years I still have on my wrists) by long braided threads. I was then instructed by the older females to 'bop' the younger girls who came near me on the head as this would ensure that they would also get married soon.

Then my mum came to braid my hair. First she oiled it, then combed it out straight and braided it from one side to the other until all the hair was one thick braid. To this she applied a sachet, sent by the groom's family, which contained wonderful-smelling fragrant herbs, each of which had a significant meaning. This was all pulled together, after which the veil was put on; it looked like I had a crown on my head. Whilst all this was going on, I sat with my face covered by my veil, being instructed by one of my elder cousins to sing a going away song! She whispered the words in my ear and I had to repeat them out loud.

The song was all about how sad I was at leaving my parents, brothers, sisters, cousins, nieces, nephews, uncles and aunts. There were special verses for the deceased and for our relatives in India. By the time my hair was done, the whole house was full of crying women and girls. There was always talk about the girls who didn't complete this ritual as 'brazen hussies, who couldn't wait to get married or didn't care about their family'. Unbelievable stuff, but thank God this tradition has now disappeared from all Indian communities, even the more traditional Bhat community.

The groom's procession arrived at seven o'clock that evening: a coachload of men and boys and a small car with four women. They were welcomed in the street by all the males from my side of the family. I was allowed a peek out of the window when the procession arrived. It's meant to be a good luck thing if it's only a peek. I couldn't see my husband-to-be but, in any case, I wouldn't have been able to see his face as his head was covered in a veil of flowers flowing down from the front of his turban!

Then the groom and his elder brother, the best man, and the females, all came up the stairs where, again, they were duly welcomed by the customary pouring of oil on each side of the door. The rest of the male guests were taken by coach to the Gurdwara where the wedding meal awaited them, and also all our other invited guests, about 250 people in total. This was a three course meal, prepared and cooked by members of my family from scratch on the day, to ensure freshness; there were no head chefs, no waiters!

The Gurdwara was set up for the 60 or 70 male guests to sleep there that night. That was how it would be done in India and they were following tradition. In the morning, breakfast was served to all, a simple meal in full Punjabi-style, with pakoras, jalebis, laduus and muttea, all washed down with hot masala chai. The afternoon meal was served after the religious wedding ceremony had taken place.

MY WEDDING DAY: 29TH JULY 1974

Thinking back, it is quite hard to remember every detail of my wedding, but some parts are inscribed in my memory and will never leave me. I remember getting up really early in the morning to see my mother standing at the foot of the bed, just looking at me. Then I saw the tears in her eyes and that started me off. I knew that I was the one person in the world who was closest to my mum. I used to do all kinds of things for her, such as writing letters on her behalf to her sister in India when her eyesight started to fail, standing up to my dad when he was being difficult with her, being there for her in all manner of little ways that only a daughter can. All this was now going to be left behind. I was going away and, although I was only going to be 50 miles away, I might as well be in another part of the world, judging by how most of my friends limited visits to their parents and left as soon as their husbands called. To counteract this, I vowed that I would tell my husband I would never ask for his permission to visit my parents, that it was my right to go whenever I wanted and for as long as I wanted, and that I did not need his approval.

The day began with my mother keeping true to tradition in denying herself food and drink until after the religious part of the ceremony had taken place. I was still in my plain red outfit from the night before and the tradition was that this was the outfit I should be married in. No makeup, only the soorma in my eyes.

My jewellery comprised my nose ring and earrings, necklace and a ring. These came from my parents and the maternal side of my family. I also wore 48 red bangles, 24 on each side. This is called a 'choora' and is symbolic for brides; the bangles always come from the maternal uncles. If no blood maternal uncle was available (none existed, or he lived too far away), then someone from the same clan as the mother (referred to as a 'cousin brother') was called upon to perform this very important function.

My veil was draped around me in such a fashion that neither my face nor any part of my hands or feet were visible. This was a special veil (called a saloo) which, again, came from the maternal side of the family. I was instructed to minimise my hand movements so that they stayed underneath the veil at all times. And I had to keep my head bowed down. When the time for the ceremony came, I was asked by the gianni to stand and walk behind my husband for the 'lava'. This entailed me sitting cross-legged on the floor in the Gurdwara, next to my husband-to-be and in front of the Guru Granth Sahib and the whole congregation. I was surrounded by a small circle of my female relatives while my husband-to-be had his aunts and grandmother sitting next to him to support and give instructions on when to get up and when to sit!

All the while, I was totally covered by this huge, heavy red veil which no-one could see through, especially the groom. Eventually, the prayers started, then the time came for my father to hand me over to my future husband. According to custom, the groom has a scarf tied over his left shoulder as part of his wedding outfit. This was unfurled and my father handed me one end of it then gave the other end to the groom. We stood up and started to perambulate the Guru Granth Sahib whilst the vows were being sung by the gianni; the groom leading and his bride following.

I couldn't see anything apart from my own feet at this point, so to help the bride, it is customary for all her male relatives to form a circle around the platform from where the scriptures are being read. In this way they were able to guide me around until I sat down. This ritual was performed four times, during which I got so hot, uncomfortable and thirsty that, every so often, someone would stick a cup of water underneath the veil and push it into my mouth. I think the whole ceremony lasted about four hours, after which we were pronounced married. I was exhausted by then!

After this part of the ceremony, I was taken home while the groom's family stayed on to have their meal. I got washed and changed out of the simple outfit into the wedding outfit which I had made myself. All the sequins were handstitched to it while sitting in my attic bedroom, looking out of the window onto the bowling green. My jewellery now consisted of all the items that had been sent by my mother-in-law and these included bangles, necklaces, rings and head ornaments. I was loaded down with all this stuff! My dowry, which had been set out for the groom's family to view, was now all packed up into a large trunk because it was getting close to the time for me to leave.

I remember going to the toilet and looking in the mirror and thinking how beautiful I looked. After that, most of the day was a blur of people coming and going around me. All sorts of rituals were being played out by the females from my side of the family, such as teasing the groom and his best man, hiding the groom's shoes and so on.

In preparation for leaving, I was taken to sit on a chair next to my mum and also our lovely Mrs. McColl, whom we'd invited just for this occasion. She was very special to me, like a surrogate granny. Now it was time for everyone to come and say goodbye – my whole family, consisting of about 70 or 80 people of all ages. They came up to me, one by one, to give me a hug and hand me some money; everyone was crying. I was so upset underneath my veil, I could hardly breathe.

The next thing I noticed was Mrs. McColl getting up. She just grabbed her walking stick, gave me a hug and a kiss and walked out. The last people to hug me were my mum and dad. I felt hugely sad and worried about my mum. I'd been her support for so long, what was she going to do without me? How would she get by, how would she write to her sister in India?

Finally, my nephew, Gurdeep, who was only a year old, was placed in my lap. I was crying because he was very close to me and I knew he would miss me a lot. Then my big brother came over and picked me up, tilted me over his shoulder and carried me out of the house, down three flights of stairs to deposit me onto the back seat of the car that the female contingent of my husband's family had arrived in the night before. No big limousine or ribbons, balloons or wedding banners, just a nice car.

My heart was thumping so much I thought everyone could hear it. Eventually, the car moved off and I continued crying for another ten minutes or so before my sister and my husband's granny calmed me down. I was still sniffing, sitting in the back seat and veiled to the hilt, but I managed to peer through and get a glimpse of my husband who was sitting in the front passenger seat. All I got was a half profile look at him, but my initial thoughts were, 'Hmm, not bad. He's quite handsome. My friends were right.'

We arrived in Edinburgh around 8 p.m. and that was the trigger for all the rituals and customs from the groom's side to take place. I have a picture of my husband and I sitting on a bed during one of the rituals and his face is glowing like the cat who's got the cream!

The next morning, July 30th, it seemed that the entire female Sikh community in Edinburgh came to see the new bride. I was given presents and my mother-in-law was praised on her newly-acquired intelligent, bilingual daughter-in-law. News of my reading and writing in Punjabi had spread very quickly and I was even asked by my mother-in-law to write in her book, in Punjabi, the gifts I was presented with, as she would have to return the favours. This was an unheard-of request, so it became a talking point for years to come.

After all the rituals had been completed, I was taken back to my parent's house where I would stay for four weeks. This was a period of rest for both families that allowed people to get things back to normal and for both the bride and groom to rest after the whole experience. I still hadn't seen my husband properly, nor he me, but suffice to say he was quietly confident that he had 'hit the jackpot', as he told me afterwards. I supposedly had won the lottery even before it existed, by all accounts, listening to my friends and cousins and going by the sneak peek that I had taken.

We arrived back in Glasgow, in the late afternoon on the 30th, to experience further rituals and customs. This time I was accompanied by my mother-in-law, my husband, his elder brother and my sister. We still had the official registration marriage to take place on the 31st of July, 1974 at Martha Street Registry Office. Even for this, I was heavily veiled so that no-one could see my face, and I had to repeat the vows through the veil. At one point I felt a bit dizzy and must have wobbled as one of my older male cousins (they always stood at the back to make sure we girls didn't wobble) came swiftly behind me and whispered in my ear, 'Stay strong, family honour is at stake.'

*

In September 1974, I moved to Edinburgh to live with my husband and his family. I continued reading from my small prayer book on a daily basis. When we finally spoke to each other, my husband said, 'I can't promise everything but I do promise that we will have a 50/50 relationship.'

He was implying that we would have an equal relationship, not like the ones we had seen where men were dominant in all things. In his own way, he was speaking of the equality that I had in my mind, the equality of Guru Nanak's teachings. We did fall in love. It was love at first sight – real love – although at that point we both had no idea of what lay ahead.

I had memorised the first five stanzas of the *Punj Pauri's of Japji Sahib*. It was very rare for anyone from the first generation of children born to immigrant Sikhs to read or write in the Gurmukhi language. There were no schools in Scotland, or in fact, the UK then, that taught Gurmukhi and the only way to learn this language was at the Gurdwara, where weekly lessons were held on Sundays. Even this facility was restricted, insofar as no girls above the age of 12 or 13 were allowed to attend these lessons, by our particular sect of the Sikh faith. So, for me, at the age of 21, to be fluent orally and in written form, in Gurmukhi, was a novelty. However, for me there was this feeling that I might be considered weird because it was mainly older people we saw and heard reading the daily prayers, either verbally by rote or from the *Gutka*.

So the minute my husband left for work at seven in the morning, I would quickly get organised and then sit on a chair behind the kitchen door and start my prayers. With one ear on the door, if I heard any movement, I would quickly get up from the chair and start doing something. I was worried that my husband's family would

69

think I was some sort of religious fanatic. Or my husband would think he had married an old woman. However, I was wrong on both counts. I became a source of pride for my in-laws as they could boast about their new addition to the family, who although born and bred in Scotland, and never having been to India, was nonetheless fluent in the Punjabi tongue. In later years my husband thought that my prayers were enough for both of us to get into heaven!

It was at this early stage in my married life that I met my now lifelong friend and confidante, Sheila Dhariwal. Sheila was a community worker who was allocated to the Sikh community to encourage and support women from ethnic groups to access local community projects. She had become friendly with my sister, Sukhwant, and would come to pick up her son, and also my younger brothers-in-law, to take them to the community centre in Leith.

I had been in Edinburgh for about four weeks when I first met Sheila, when she had come to pick up the boys as usual, and I answered the door. She says that she vividly remembers her surprise at seeing a 'young woman dressed in turquoise and wearing turquoise eye shadow'. She became my link to the outside world; I could talk with her of 'other things in life' and we are still friends to this day.

But my spiritual journey really began in 1979, when I was 25 years old and the mother of two boys. My husband's grandmother, Inder Kaur, had come from India at the time of Partition and had lived in Edinburgh all her life. She had no sons and her husband had died in the late 50s, leaving her to live the best part of 50 years on her own. She was well supported by her two daughters – (one was my mother-in-law) – and their families, and had become the doyen of the family. She commanded respect from both males and females. She was my role model – she had an inner strength to stand up to people, to be fearless.

Being on her own led her to read from the scriptures also, but she would say that she didn't take it further than reading at home. She was impressed by my aptitude to read Gurmukhi at such a young age. So, in 1979, when my husband had gone on his journey with the Merchant Navy, Granny decided that she would help to keep my mind occupied. She had a Janam Sakhi (Janam Sakhi literally means a 'Birth Story') about Guru Nanak's life and times.

Granny had brought this copy with her when she had left India in the late 40s. She persuaded me to come and read to her as she felt this would help me pass the time and it would give her peace of mind. Every evening, after I had finished my household duties, I would go upstairs to her wee flat. She lived on the topmost floor of the same tenement that we stayed in, in Antigua Street.

When I read the Janam Sakhi for the the first time, I really didn't understand what I was reading – the words didn't make sense to me and I could not fully understand the meanings. I must have read the whole Janam Sakhi at least three times before I slowly began to understand and make sense of the words and sentences. They were written in poetic form and it was difficult to comprehend what I was reading about! These sessions began to give me confidence in reading out loud. Before, I had always read silently, afraid of making mistakes.

Gradually, it also became more apparent to me that Sikhism, or being a Sikh, did not mean that it was wrong to have dreams and ambitions or that, as a Sikh woman, I should be denied the same rights as Sikh men. In fact, it became quite clear that being a follower of Guru Nanak's path of spiritualism and doctrine of equality was the essence of being a Sikh. The rules and regulations, the internal societal barriers, which now prevailed within our community in the second half of the 20th century, had all been made by the males of the community, and were designed specifically to control the women of that community. They were in direct contravention of Guru Nanak's original tenet. Guru Nanak viewed the role of women in society as equal to that of men in all aspects of the Sikh faith, from reading the scriptures to running the Gurdwaras.

Women born into the Bhat sect of the Sikh faith were particularly affected by these hidden codes of conduct. We always had to cover our faces in the presence of males who were senior to our husbands, even in the Gurdwara. Yet Guru Nanak had forbidden this practice and the scriptures state that no woman should enter the Gurdwara with her face covered.

I desperately wanted to read more from the scriptures and to speak to, and learn from, the giannis who came to the Gurdwara. I wanted to know the meanings of what was being read, but there was no one to speak to and I was not allowed to do this. So my internal battle continued. I read at home and prayed that God would hear me.

In 1981, a visiting gianni came to Edinburgh and confronted the whole community as to why there were no women reading from the scriptures. He asked why all the women were still sitting with their faces covered in God's house? Could the elders not see that this was totally against Guru Nanak's message? He challenged all the elders in the community, asking them to look within their families to see if there were any females who could read Gurmukhi fluently. If there were, he asked that they be brought to the Gurdwara where he would assess their ability and support them to take the first steps in reading aloud from the Guru Granth Sahib, in front of the congregation. I couldn't believe my ears. The first thing that went through my mind was, 'There is a God, he's heard my prayers.'

My husband was fine with me going along to the Gurdwara, but only if the elders in the family would agree to it. The elders were unhappy about the situation, worrying what adverse effect it would have on the other daughters-in-law in the family. The deciding factor was that they would have been considered dishonourable if they stopped me from reading the Holy Scriptures, and they did not want to be labelled like that.

The next day, I was given permission to be assessed. I was very apprehensive – I was sitting next to a total stranger, and a man at that! I did my reading and he listened intently. When I had finished, he looked at me and my mother-in-law, who was my chaperone, and said, 'Tomorrow, I will start this young woman on her path of reading from the Guru Granth Sahib.'

I was both shocked and elated. There *was* a God. He had heard my prayers. He believed in me. I was sure that He had sent me here for a purpose other than cooking and cleaning!

The following day, at the Gurdwara, the gianni called me up to the dais in front of the podium on which the Granth Sahib is positioned, and where the gianni sits to read. He read Ardass (a prayer of blessings) to give me strength and courage to begin my reading of the Holy Scriptures. He led me onto the podium and seated me, then I started to read. The words just floated in front of me, my head was pounding and my face became very red and hot. I probably read for 15 minutes, yet it seemed like a lifetime. I have also had the privilege of reading from the Granth Sahib in India, at our family gathering when we visited in 2009.

Once I had become established as part of the reading group who took part in the three day readings, on special occasions at our Gurdwara in Edinburgh, I was put on the rota and sometimes my reading slot would be at four o'clock in the morning. I couldn't drive at that time so would have to wake my husband up to drop me off. He never complained out loud but there were smatterings of mutterings under his breath – 'Why do you have to be Miss Holy-Moly?'

Secretly, he was very proud, but he rarely showed it in those early days. I think he was worried that I might become too religious and forsake my duties as a wife and mother.

I then went on a mission to pass my driving test because then I would not have to disturb anyone and could drive myself to the Gurdwara at any time in the morning. I had been taking driving lessons before I got married – my big brother had been my instructor. But everything stopped when my mother decided that I was going to get married and it would be better all round if I completed this driving business in Edinburgh.

As was the custom in those days, once married, I was at the mercy of decisions made by the elders in the family. There was never a direct 'no', and in a roundabout way my husband was advised that he could give his wife driving lessons. But it was important that his younger brothers be given priority as they would be going out to work. So my lessons happened – some with my husband, some with driving schools and some with my nephew, Kirtan, who was only five when I got married. But never had I reached the stage of a test.

In 1993, I decided that I was going to go for it. I enrolled with the British School of Motoring and took the advice of a neighbour who was in the process of becoming a driving instructor himself. He said, 'When the instructor asks if you have been practicing outwith the lessons, say yes, even if you haven't. It will help with you getting booked for a test quicker.' I took his advice and at the end of my ten week block, I was booked in for my test.

On the day of the test, I didn't tell anyone. Internally, I had decided that if there was a God and he really wanted me to continue reading, he would be with me and I would pass first time. I asked my mother-in-law if she could come round and babysit as my husband was working that morning. I made up an excuse to everyone, including my husband, that I had a hospital appointment.

The driving instructor picked me up from the end of my street and off I went to Joppa, to the test centre. I had read the Highway Code and tried to memorise everything, which was nigh impossible, but I tried. The driving instructor was at least six feet tall with a long beard: very quiet, even gloomy-looking, which frightened the living daylights out of me. I continued to pray under my breath. We got off to a bad start when he said, 'At the first corner, take a left.'

I drove straight ahead, stopped with a jolt and turned to ask him what he had said! He kept a completely straight face and said, 'Just drive ahead and take the next right.'

The remainder of the driving seemed to go okay, and then he stopped to ask me the questions on the Highway Code. I think I answered these okay until he started showing me the cards with all the road signs and my mind went completely blank. He showed me about ten cards and I got all of them wrong, apart from the one showing animals crossing! Well, I thought, 'That's it, I'm dead now, he is not going to give me a pass.'

I was wrong, my prayers were heard and he turned to me, still with the straightest face – no smile, nothing – and said, 'I can say you have passed your test.'

There has never been anything that has surprised me more, or given me such a feeling of absolute joy, than that moment. I was ecstatic. I phoned my husband and said, 'I've passed my test!'

He was dumbfounded. He kept asking me what I was going on about, then I could hear his colleagues in the background asking if everything was okay. I could hear him saying, 'It's my wife. She says she's just passed her driving test first time!'

4

My Husband, Johnny

Johnny (his full name was Harpajin Europe Singh Kusbia) was my soulmate, with whom I shared an extraordinary life and relationship for 42 years. On March 29th 2015 he was diagnosed with pancreatic cancer and told that he had six months to live. In fact, he passed away at home, ten months later, on Friday 5th February 2016. I thought my life had ended when he passed away, but I was wrong. I slowly began to realise that I could sense him around me. I feel his presence but this does not take away the pain of not seeing him in a physical way. He is still very much a part of my soul and lives within my heart. My children had a bench made for me after he passed away and they put an inscription on it:

Johnny and Trishna

Always together never apart,

Maybe in distance never in Heart

He was born on the 31st December 1954 in Malviya Nagar, New Delhi, India. His first given name, Harpajin, means 'A devotee absorbed in the Lord'. His middle name, Europe, was ascribed to him because he was conceived just after his father had returned from his travels in Great Britain which, to the people of India, was Europe or 'Vailat'. He was given the name Johnny or John in his childhood since his friends found Harpajin difficult to pronounce. The name, Johnny, also more accurately reflected his mischievous nature.

I asked him many times to write down his life story but he would always reply, 'You do it.'

I used to think, 'No, why should I do it? Why don't you do it yourself?'

I always encouraged and tried to persuade him to take part in various Sikh projects that came up: about the history of Leith, its diverse cultures, the Sikh community in Leith, but he just would not participate. However, he did consent to take part in one particular project, in February 2015. This project was being delivered by another community group (MECCOP) and they were seeking to collate stories of two generations of family – Mothers and Daughters/ Fathers and Sons.

I had been asked to try and recruit people from the Sikh Community, but Sikhs are often reluctant to take part in these types of projects, an attitude that other communities sometimes find difficult to understand. I think there's an inherent fear in Sikhs of being public about their lives. They don't see the benefits of participation in cross-community communications, that their story could be inspiring within the Sikh communities, and provide knowledge and understanding of the history and customs of their own particular sect to other communities. However, that observation aside, Johnny agreed to participate, together with my younger son, Dilal, even though he was unwell at this stage – although he had not yet been diagnosed with cancer.

What follows is his account and then Dilal's, which appear in the book *Mothers and Daughters, Fathers and Sons* edited by Emma-Jane Harrington, Suzanne Munday and Peter E Ross.

'My name is Harpajin John Singh, I was born in New Delhi, India. The first memories of my home life started in Tennant Street, Leith, Edinburgh. It was so integrated, the whole community. It didn't matter who you were, what colour you were, what nationality you were, everybody got on like a house on fire. The doors would be open, everybody could walk in and out, there was no fear, no resentment, everybody knew each other and respected each other, which was the most important thing. I had both Indian and Scottish friends, they were both equal to me. If I was speaking with my Indian friends we would speak Indian, if I was with my Scottish lads, I'd be talking pure Leith – a totally different accent to Edinburgh, it's a unique, individual, independent accent, that's why we were called 'Leithers'. We went to Bonnington Primary school and the annexe was called Dr Bell's. I used to wear the full Sikh regalia, long hair in a top knot on my head, then I started wearing the turban.

I lost my father when I was ten years old, in a road traffic accident. My mother brought up eight children on her own. My mother was so close to me. We've just lost her, she was 90 years old. (*John's mum, Harbans Kaur, passed away on 3rd April 2015, four days after he was diagnosed with cancer*). My mother never worked. The only thing she got from the government was child benefit and a widow's pension. That's what she got, so we barely survived but we did survive. The neighbours were so nice and within that street there were about four or five Asian families. No, I'd say about seven, 'cause there were some Pakistani families and the rest were Sikh families. We got on so great, there was no hassle even though there was friction between the two countries – we were like that.

I was a paper boy in the morning, a paper boy after school and a milk boy in the morning as well, six days a week. I was about ten years old. The milk thing was on a three-wheeler milk float and the guy's name was John. He had about four workers and we knew the system like the back of our hand: first floor, second floor, third floor, left-hand side, right-hand side, Mrs. Smith, Mr. Thomson, this thing, that thing. I used to make sure there was extra milk on the float to give to these elderly people.

Saturday was the best day of the week, there used to be weddings on a Saturday. We would tick off between four to six churches with weddings going on. We'd be running from one wedding for the 'pour-out' where they used to throw the money – and God, when you used to come home, your legs were all battered and bruised and scraped and scratched but you thought nothing of it. The money you made you couldn't spend, so you would give your mother some money and keep some for yourself for sweets, chocolates. Ice-cream, pop, all that kinda stuff.

Our New Year is called 'Vaisakhi'. That comes in April and it's huge. All the community would get together in the Gurdwara. There would be the spiritual side of it and once the spiritual side was over there was vegetarian food. After the food we would tidy up the temple, the kitchen and the rooms. Then each family would go back to their own homes and families would invite other families that evening for a party. If you never had any brothers or sisters within your vicinity, you would get asked anyway – 'We can't leave so-and-so, that's not nice, that's not fair, his family is back home in India so we'll make him welcome here.' That kept communities so bonded it was unbelievable.

There were nine of us, including my mother. We struggled, we really struggled. We stayed in two rooms and there was a kitchen. We had bunk beds on top of bunk beds and a mattress on the floor just to make ends meet. So that was the type of living standard we had, but there was always food on the table; we always tried to earn an honest bob, earn enough money to get on with it. My big brother worked as a labourer until he got married at nineteen. Well, I lost my dad in 1964, my brother got married in 1967 and then he and his wife had a child. That was another addition to the family.

In 1970 my elder brother and I were working and we had saved enough money to buy a bigger house in Antigua Street at the top of Leith Walk, above the Deep Sea chip shop. As I got older, in my teens, there was no discrimination. I've never experienced it. My Scottish lads friends, they never looked at me as, 'Oh he's got a turban on.' I could speak the lingo, the language, pure Leith. As far as they were concerned, 'That's Johnny Singh, he's just one of the boys that's it, end of story.' So your features, your turban, your appearance didn't bother anybody, never bothered nobody.

I thoroughly enjoyed my time at Bellevue secondary school[5]. Academically, I came out with a Edinburgh Schools Certificate. The last week of school we had a careers guidance meeting. I was mechanically minded and someone suggested I try the shipyards.

My first job was as an apprentice TV aerial rigger but the thought of standing on chimney pots, 80 or 90 feet up, put the fear of death into me. So I stopped that, left on a Friday and got an interview with Robb Caledon Shipbuilders. I wanted to be a welder but I was good with my hands so they put me in the engineering department where I became a marine engineer. I started my apprenticeship on the Monday with my turban intact. I was 15.

The first year you're just a wee message laddie, but you're still picking up things. I had my five year apprenticeship. The theory was at Telford College day release. I completed the apprenticeship and got my City and Guilds in Mechanical Engineering. I was about 17 when, to my mum's dismay, I had my hair cut as I thought it might hamper my career going forward. I joined the Merchant Navy and worked on oil tankers that were 300,000 tons. We would cycle to get from the stern to the bow of the ship. I worked on ships that would test drill for oil companies. That was worldwide, taking me to the Mediterranean, Hong Kong and the Persian Gulf. I left this after about seven years and moved on to a company that was involved in shutting down the power stations like Torness, Cockenzie, Longgannet and Hunterston. In 2000 I took a change in my career and started work

5   *The school was on London Street – Bellevue Secondary School, now renamed Drummond Community School. The head teacher was a Mr. Dunn.*

within the voluntary sector and got a job with an organisation called Skillnet who were helping men from ethnic communities back into employment. I retired from there in 2010.

I really wanted to be a professional football player, the first Sikh football player. That was my goal, not to be big-headed, I was very good! Ninety-nine percent was football and one percent we were naughty lads, very naughty lads!

Now that I am older, now I really miss my father. Had he been here, God knows what my life would have been like. But we've got a saying in our culture: there is a purpose for a human being to be here, we call it 'kismet'. Kismet means it's written down for you. You are born, you come with nothing, you go with nothing.'

The following is Dilal's story:

'My name is Dilal Singh and I am 32 years old. I stayed in Rosslyn Crescent, it's got a big plantation in the middle of the street – a grassy pitch with a wee wall round it. We played fitball from a tree and a wall. My childhood was brilliant because of the street. There were a lot of kids my age so every day was just fun, because we had the 'planny' we were safe. You didnae think of anything, never had any thoughts, no worries, nae nothin.

There is a photo of my brother Terry's wedding, nearly twenty five years ago, and it's got every child in our family at the bottom of this plantation. Look at that photo – that will show you. That's the squad, like, of just our family. Then you had all the kids fae the street, they arenae in the photo but it will give you an idea of the amount of numbers that am talking aboot.

I've always wanted money. I used to buy sweets in the morning in primary school and sell them in the playground, so I would have more money at the end of the day to buy a bigger ice cream. I was working at 15 while I was at school – I was peeling tatties in my cousin Tony Singh's restaurant. It was one of the best restaurants in

Edinburgh at the time, Olorosso.

I used to sit through the back with one of my pals fae school, peeling tatties. We would walk through the restaurant with our school bags and I'd be like, 'One day am going to be sitting here.'

When I was 18 years old I went up, wearing a suit, got a bottle of champagne and sat on the terrace on an absolute scorcher of a day with my friends. It was an absolute stoater of a day.

For me, money was a lot. I don't know why though, because I didnae go withoot. But now am different. I'm the complete opposite. Everything's so instant, so fast, life's too fast right now. That's one of the reasons I dinnae like money. Cos when you're running a business your life goes rapid. And if ye dinnae enjoy what you're daein before you know it, it's gone.

When I was growing up everybody wanted to be a fitball player, but am tiny. I'm five foot, I'm not going to be a fitball player. I knew that, quickly tae. But I was good at it, I loved it. I was like an underdog, naebody thought I could play fitball but when I played, I played properly, I played well. I wasnae scoring goals, I was making my team win. Music was a part of the hoose. My brother, cause he was so much older than us, whatever he listened tae, we listened tae. I used to listen to The Specials, Bob Marley and then mid 90s trance, techno. Then my sister, Radha, dictated what music we were allowed to listen tae because my mum and dad didnae know really about the culture, what was going, they were away fae that. But music in the hoose was a big deal. All my uncles were into music, they all had big vinyls and records. They were into all their soul stuff, Sam Cooke, all the good stuff.

Me and my sister got on well, we both liked hip-hop. As every young boy, I loved the swearing and all that stuff!'

*

Johnny was different from all the other Asian/Sikh men of his generation in Edinburgh. Even in Glasgow, he was an enigma and a fashion icon. He had his hair cut at the age of 17; he was very handsome, very light-skinned and looked more Italian or white. He wore this statement on his back: he would never wear the same shirt twice in one week. He always had the latest fashion item, such as cheesecloth shirts, polo necks, bell bottom trousers (the width had to be 17 inches!) His hair was washed and blow-dried every day. This was all before we were married, and when we were married, I became his personal hairdresser.

He taught me how to hold the hairbrush and twirl it around and then hold the hairdryer close and dry! I became his trophy wife when he walked down the street, he wanted people to see him as a successful man of the world. Not an Asian/Sikh, even though he was very proud of his heritage. He wanted women to fancy him and men to envy him and by George, they did!

In fact, in 1988, on our first visit to India, my mum's sister met us both for the first time and was quite taken by him. She thought that as I was a British-born Sikh, I had been allowed to make my own choice and had married a white man. I was in stitches, but also taken aback at how we, the first-generation people born and raised in the UK, were viewed by our relatives in India in those days. They automatically assumed that we had lost our tradition and did not expect us to have carried on with outdated rituals and customs, not realising how wrong they were.

Johnny's interpretation of being 'a naughty schoolboy' was something of an understatement as I found out just after our marriage. We had been married for about two months and two of John's younger brothers had been suspended from school. My mother-in-law was asked to go to their school to meet with the headmaster. I was to accompany her because she could not speak English and needed someone to translate. We arrived and were taken to the headmaster's office.

He was a very stern-looking man; he had his black gown on and was leaning back in his chair. He proceeded to relate the reason for suspension and then realised that he did not know who I was. I introduced myself as the new sister-in-law, married to the elder brother of said culprits. He looked at me then asked which brother. I said, 'Johnny Singh,' adding, 'I think he was at this school also.'

That was too much for the man. He just leaned right back in his chair and said, 'You can't possibly be married to Johnny Singh, he was a rascal. How did he manage to get married to someone as intelligent and beautiful as you? I'm speechless. I never thought he would do anything with his life. He was always in trouble, either causing it or involved in the thick of it. You are married to him, are you sure?'

This happened 46 years ago, yet I still have not forgotten the look on that headmaster's face as he actually walked us all the way back from his office to the gates. All along, he just kept smiling at me and nodding his head in disbelief.

Johnny qualified as a Marine Engineer and continued working in the shipyards for a further two years. He then enrolled in the Merchant Navy and went to sea in 1979. This was an adventure that didn't last very long: he became homesick, and being away from home for three months at a time did not suit him or his lifestyle! It also did not suit me when it had first been discussed. I was totally against it as I and our two sons would miss him terribly. I didn't want to be sitting at home while he was having a jaunty time on the high seas. But he was so desperate to go that I began to think, perhaps I should let him. I didn't want to be someone whom he'd resent for holding him back from his dream.

I gave permission and off he went, but now we were in a very different space. So when he started phoning home to say he was really not happy and was becoming quite ill with the worry of having to stay on board for a further three months, I was not particularly sympathetic. However, I was instructed by my mother-in-law to get him home at all costs. I didn't have a clue what to do or who to speak to but eventually I decided to speak with my doctor. She was a lovely person and understood my dilemma. She instructed me to contact the ship's captain and inform him that I was under pressure, looking after the children and extended family, to the extent that my doctor was worried that it would impact on my mental health. She produced a medical certificate for me to send and because of this, my husband was given an early discharge. On his return, he immediately went offshore to the oil rigs for a period. On one occasion he told me he was going to Aberdeen but he actually flew out to Gibraltar. I only found out after he had been, when my present from Aberdeen was the most beautiful handmade silk housecoat I had ever seen. He then joined British Rail as a fitter and was in that job until 1984.

Above left: John aged 3

Above right: My dad and my mum's big brother

Below left: Diwali 1965, family in McCulloch St.

Below right: My dad, mum, paternal granny, Besant-Kaur, me as a baby

Above: Family portrait taken in 1964/65 Diwali L-R My dad, me, my mum, my sister, Ashan, my eldest brother, Gurdev. Seated L-R My wee brothers Chander, Subash and Gadraj

Below: Sant Fateh Singh, seated, was an Indian Sikh religious and political leader. He visited Glasgow in 1969. R-L My mum with Dad standing behind her.
Standing on the left is my Mum's brother, Ajagar Singh, and first right is my mum's sister, Jeeva Kaur

Above: My dad welcoming a famous Bollywood actor to Glasgow

Below: South Portland Street Glasgow Gurdwara in 1958/9
Seated on the floor L-R: I am in the plain jumper looking at the camera, my sister, Sukhwant, in striped cardi, and my sister, Ashan, looking at my brother, Gurdev, seated in a cousin's lap. My dad is on the right, seated with my brother, Subash, in his lap. We were already making history. We were the only girls in that pic!

Above: 1989 family pic with Rajvinder, Neelam, Dilal in Johnny's lap and Radha hiding in the back

Middle: 40 McCulloch St. My brother, Subash's wedding.

Below: My mum and her elder brother's wife

Above left: Me, my dad, my brother, Chander, and Sukwant and her children

Above right: L-R Me, my newly-married sister, Ashan, my sister-in-law, Ravinder and my mum

Middle: McCulloch St back garden with Ashan and Ravinder

Below: 1974 The three of us were visiting Glasgow and we were on a day trip to Luss. I had been married for about 3 months

Above: 2001 The birth of our grandson, Jeevan. L-R My son, Rajvinder, his wife, Sharon, my mother-in-law, Harbans, me with baby Jeevan and John

Below: Our wedding day. We had arrived in Edinburgh on the 29th of July. My husband would say he felt like 'the cat who had got the cream'. I am under the red veil!

Above: 2007. My graduation from Glagow University

Right: 2009 India, Shimla

Below: 1997. John and I at St James's Palace. Celebration of 50 years of the Commonwealth

Above: Family

Middle: 2014. Glasgow Sikh Community Awards, John and I

Below: 2010. At the opening of our Social Enterprise Punjab'n De Rasoi. John had the plaque made for us in India

Above: 1988 Our first visit to India

Below: Family trip to Buckingham Palace

Above: Me reading from the Guru Granth Sahib at the Edinburgh Gurdwara.

Middle: Punjabi Junction cafe with John

Below: Me and my granddaughter, Amahn, Holyrood Palace

5

1984

In this cataclysmic year for us, I was a married woman of ten years with two sons: Rajvinder Terry Singh who was nine years old at the time, and Ameet Rungu Andrew Singh, who would be six in August that year. My first daughter, Radha, was also conceived in that year.

Mentally, I was in a state of turmoil at that time. I was constantly driven by a desire, an ambition, to be more than just a wife and mother, but there was more than that; I knew that I was living a life that was not aligned with the Sikh ethos or insight.

Then, on June 4th 1984 in India, 3000 miles away, an atrocity was perpertrated. The Golden Temple, the holiest Sikh shrine, was stormed by the Indian Army in an attack code-named Operation Blue Star. The aim was to flush out so-called Sikh separatists, and this act changed the lives of Sikhs forever. Indeed, the repercussions and pain of those events have remained with those who experienced it, both directly and from afar, to this day. It was the biggest tragedy for the worldwide community of Sikhs in the 20th century. It left an indelible scar on their psyche.

At 4 a.m. the army started to shell the Gurdwara Complex, in particular the historic Ramgarhia Bungas, the water tank and other fortified positions, with no warning whatsoever. Thousands of innocent worshippers of all ages were trapped inside. According to the British newspaper, *The Times*, 'A doctor told journalists that bodies of victims were brought to the mortuary by police in municipal refuse lorries. There were reports that, of the 400 bodies, 100 were women and between 15 to 20 were children under five.'

This shocking attack affected the whole Sikh nation worldwide. But my family endured its own heart-breaking tragedy at this time which would have an even more devastating and lifelong effect on our lives. At six o'clock on the same morning as that assault on the Golden Shrine, I was waiting for my husband to return from his night shift at the British Rail works depot in Craigentinny. But he had decided to go for a drink with some of his mates, so he didn't get home until 10ish and was asleep by the time I got back from dropping the boys off at their school. Normally, he would have got up around three then made himself something to eat. I would leave the house at three to pick up the boys from school so that, by the time we got home, he would be waiting with a cup of tea and ready to listen to the boys' day at school.

But when we came home that day, he wasn't up which annoyed me. I went into the bedroom and asked him if he was getting up to get ready for work. He mumbled from under the covers, 'I'm not going into work today.'

That made me really angry. He had gone drinking early, was now unfit to do anything meaningful so all our plans were wrecked. Just then the phone rang – my elder sister, Sukhwant, said she was going round to my mother-in-law's with her kids (we shared the same mother-in-law, she being married to my husband's eldest brother) – did I want to join her?

I normally never went out with the kids once they were home from school. They had homework to do and would usually spend some time with their dad before he went on his night shift. But this time I said, 'Yes, I'll come. I'll meet you round there.' We lived in Elm Row at that time and my mother-in-law lived in Antigua Street, about a five minute walk away. It's on the west side of Leith Walk, from the south-east corner of Union Street going north-eastwards to Gayfield

Square. I got the boys changed out of their uniforms and said, 'Let's go, Dad can sleep it off, we're going to Granny's for a bit.' Both were surprised as it wasn't something we did during the week.

When we got to my mother-in-law's, my sister was already there with her two younger kids and my other sister, Ashan, who also lived in nearby Albert Street, with her three children. Both my sisters-in-law lived in the same house, together with their four children. So with 11 young kids all charging about the same house, there was an awful lot of noise being made! My mother-in-law was quite stressed that day and seemed annoyed that we had all turned up unannounced. I sensed her agitation, and that made me do something that I never normally would. I said to the boys, 'Go down to Gayfield Square Park and play with the other kids there.'

They both ran off. About 20 minutes later, there was a banging on the front door and when I opened it, there was one of my husband's nieces. She was screaming, 'Come down quick, Rungu's been hit by a car.' I remember running down the stairs, cursing and swearing at the boys, saying, 'They'll be the death of me. I bet he's broken a leg or something.' My mother-in-law and sisters were behind me, all shouting at me, saying, 'Don't run, you're pregnant. Be careful, he'll be fine.'

I don't remember who called my husband because there were no mobiles in those days. But by the time I reached the park he was already there, kneeling beside my son. Neither of us knew what to do. The car had hit him, thrown him up and he had landed in front of it. Rajvinder later recalled that they had both come out of the gate and started to cross the small road in front of Gayfield Square Police Station when the car involved had come speeding round the corner and hit Rungu. We both rode with Rungu in the ambulance to the Royal Infirmary which at that time was still in Lauriston Place. We were given a small private room to wait in while various doctors came and went. Scans were taken and tests done. Eventually, somebody came to tell us that there was swelling on Rungu's brain and that meant they would have to sedate him until they could do further tests.

My mother, mother-in-law, my husband's grandmother, my sister and I all stayed at the hospital for seven days. Every day I prayed to God to save my son. At some point he went into a coma and had to be put on a ventilator to help him breathe and stay alive. Then the consultant told us that, even if he did come round, there would be severe, permanent brain damage. We, John and I, simply did not know how to cope with this. I couldn't find it in me to tell them to take him off the ventilator, while my husband just closed off completely.

On Tuesday, June 12th my mother and mother-in-law insisted that I keep my ante-natal appointment, my first for this pregnancy, at the Elsie Inglis Hospital. I went on my own. They informed me that my child would be born around the 23rd or 24th of December. I rushed back from there to the Royal Infirmary, to find everybody standing in the corridor outside my son's ward, crying. My husband himself was numb, and dumb with grief. I pushed past them all, screaming for them to stop, that my son was fine, he couldn't be dead! I went into the room to find that they had wrapped him in some kind of foil. I pulled everything off him but he was cold. His body had given up. The brain damage had affected everything and his organs had failed. After that, everything was a blur. I think my husband went into deep shock right there and then, but neither he nor I realised it until much later. For him, it brought back flashbacks of his father's death which had also been a tragic car accident.

I then had to deal with all the cultural rituals which, when I look back, were so horrible and often insensitive that I can't believe I went along with them. The funeral was arranged for the 15th of June but that date is a major festival (Thumdey) for the Bhat community. One of the older women from the community contacted my mother-in-

100

law and said, 'You can't have the funeral on that day, people will not come.' So the funeral was moved to the 16th of June.

I was shocked by this, but felt I couldn't say anything. In fact, the hurt went even deeper. There are certain rituals that happen on this festival and the convention was that, if we as a family didn't conduct those rituals on that day, we would not be permitted to celebrate this festival in future. I stood in shock as my mother-in-law insisted that I take part in the rituals. My son had died, he was still lying in the mortuary and here I was, being forced to take part in some unnecessary stuff that had no rhyme nor reason. I still feel pain every time this festival comes round as it reminds me of 1984.

When the coffin was brought up the stairs into our house, I stood there, looking at him, screaming and crying. One of my husband's aunts said of me, 'She's not covering her face with her veil, yet there are many elder men here!' That bitter memory has lived with me ever since: my son had died, yet all this woman was concerned about was that my face wasn't covered. Furthermore, the elders in the family decided that, as I was pregnant, I couldn't go with them to scatter his ashes. To this day, I don't know where they took them. I also don't know if my husband went with them or not. We never spoke about it as it was always too painful. After my husband passed away in 2016, I wanted to know where my son's ashes were scattered and I asked elder members of the family but no one could remember.

We were not allowed to have a memorial service for him because he was a child so he had 'gone back to spirit'. As time went on, I could never say that my son was dead. In fact, I just didn't talk about it to anyone. I felt guilty that there we were, living our lives, while he was gone, just disappeared in a flash.

This point marked the beginning of my husband's depression which in turn led to Post Traumatic Stress Disorder – but this remained undiagnosed until 2014 – 30 years later and just two years before he died. For myself, I found that all the rituals I had been going through during the period of mourning made no sense. They were not followed for religious reasons, they were all cultural, from ages gone by. They represented what was done in the villages, which was in fact a mix of Hindu/Muslim ritual. This made me angry and I felt no one was listening to me when I asked why.

I was told the same thing over and over: it's what is done. There was no one who could explain to me why. Both of my sisters were older than me but they also just went along with whatever was being instructed by the elders.

I began to focus on reading from the Guru Granth Sahib scriptures and this, I found, helped me get through the most difficult time in my life. The more I read, the more I came to understand that we had been living a life that was entrenched in ritual, customs that had no link whatsoever with our religious teachings. The scriptures talked of equality, kindness, and humanity, of not being trapped in rituals but instead of living life free of things that trapped the mind into false belief systems.

My son, Rajvinder, was deeply affected by seeing his brother knocked down. This is his account of the repercussions of that day:

'Being with my brother and witnessing first-hand the car accident that resulted in his death is something that will never leave me. There is never a day where my brother is not in my thoughts, and I still to this day see him clearly being struck by the car immediately after I let go of his hand to cross the road. The impact of this trauma caused me indescribable pain, guilt and anger. We were inseparable and I have wonderful memories of when we were both at London Street Primary School and of playing together at home.

My parents, uncles and extended family did everything they could to support me through my childhood and I know I was loved, and they each did the best they could to help me through the loss of my brother. PTSD and trauma were not subject matters that were commonly talked about in the eighties, along with the impact on an individual's mental health or mental health in general. Furthermore, the mention of mental health in the Sikh Community is and was something of a taboo subject and immediately brought about a degree of discomfort and stereotypical judgements that it was deemed best not to mention at all.

I assumed responsibility for my brother's death and the subsequent impact this had on my parents and extended family. I look back and can see that due to taking on this responsibility, I actively made decisions about my life that would not cause any further pain or conflict in my family's life and subconsciously took on a caring role for those around me. In my own mind I thought that this could mitigate the impact of the loss of my brother, however over time I realised that there was nothing I could do that would remove the trauma and grief of others.

Along with my family, two of the biggest influences in my life have been Shri Guru Nanak Dev Ji and Mata Yogananda Ji. Trying to live my life though selfless service to others – Sewa (pronounced Say-vaah) – and incorporating the wisdom and practice of meditation into how I approach each part of my life, has helped me to work towards resolving the inner conflict, guilt and pain caused by the loss of my brother and impact upon my family. I've also been able to find some peace within myself as I know that ultimately what happened to my brother was an accident.

I have always felt a deep desire, even as a child, to ensure that everyone was included and never left behind. I have always felt passionate and committed to sharing learning and knowledge to empower others, particularly those who are invisible, oppressed, voiceless or marginalised, to fulfil their potential and to never shy away from being themselves. I hope that this book and the experiences my mum is sharing of her life, my father's life, of the Sikh Community in Scotland and the teachings of Sikhi are able to positively influence others and encourage us all to let our own light shine.'

*

On the 31st of October 1984, the Indian Prime Minister, Mrs. Gandhi, was assassinated by her two Sikh bodyguards in revenge for Operation Bluestar. What followed beggared belief. Thousands of Sikhs were massacred by that most barbaric method, burning. Mobs were assembled to carry out a three-day orgy of killings and plunder. Almost 3000 Sikhs were murdered in four days, most of them in broad daylight, in India's capital city.

In November that year, my first cousin and his two sons were amongst the many Sikhs dragged from their homes. Tyres were put on them, kerosene poured over them, then they were burned to death in front of their other children, wife and relatives. At the time I was heavily pregnant and still in shock from the loss of my own son. However, the elder women in my family deemed it my duty to pay my respects to the family of the deceased, who lived in Glasgow.

My husband was not in any fit state to attend so he was given 'pardon'. I wasn't even given a choice! It was as though I was automatically deemed the stronger one. But this assumption that I, and not my husband, should be the one to shoulder any emotional stress became a familiar pattern in future years. In effect, it was 'don't mention it in front of your husband.' I would think, 'Why are they protecting him but not me?'

Rungu died in June, 1984, but it would be November of that year before I began to understand the extent of pain and anguish that mothers go through following the loss of a child. This recognition changed me and prompted me to look hard at what I had been thinking for most of my life. Where had I come from? Where was I heading?

I had always watched events around me from the sidelines, usually silently, wondering how other people did things, where did they get their strength from? Was I always just going to wait, passively, for 'someone' to do something for me, to change the way I led my life? But a few more years would elapse before I felt the seismic shift in my persona that catalysed within me the spirit of definitive and decisive action.

SELF-REALISATION

Reading from the Sikh scriptures helped me and my faith became my lifeline. I was looking for answers, but no one could talk to me about the scriptures. I began to see that following blindly without questioning was not helping me. I began to unpick the teachings that had been passed down to me verbally, the rituals and cultural nuances that had been woven into the words from the Guru Granth Sahib, and I found that the essence of spirituality was at the core of Sikhism. There were times when I still questioned myself and my understanding of being a Sikh and following the written words within the Guru Granth Sahib scriptures. I persevered with my reading of the scriptures as much as I could. I read and reread the Janamsakhi of Guru Nanak to understand his message of equality and service to all humankind, not to judge from whence they came, which religion they followed, which caste or race they came from.

In the early 90s my eldest son, Rajvinder, had become interested in the Self-Realisation Meditation Healing Centre in Somerset. This centre was brought into being by Mata Yogananda Mahasaya Dharma and her husband, Peter Sevananda, in 1988. It was based on the teaching of Parmahansa Yogananda, a spiritual teacher who had gone to America from India, in 1920, to spread the word of India's ancient science of Yoga, the science of knowing the Self, of realizing and experiencing who we truly are, divine souls with unlimited potential. His best-selling classic, *Autobiography of a Yogi*, continues to be the definitive introduction to yoga meditation for millions of seekers around the globe.

I, and in particular, my husband, had become quite worried – we thought Rajvinder was joining some sort of cult. Our biggest fear was, what were they teaching him? Would he move away from his Sikh roots? Were they converting him to Christianity? All the books were quite intense and sometimes I would flick through them and see references to 'Christ consciousness'. I never read them properly, which was a mistake on my part in those early days. Hence the panic and thoughts of, 'Oh my God, what's happening to my son?'

So, in 1995, when my son asked me what I wanted for Mother's Day that year, I said. 'Take me to your self-realisation place in Somerset. I want see what it's about.'

He laughed and said, 'Okay, if that's what you want.'

He booked us both a weekend retreat and off we went. We had been to London many times but had never travelled on the Tube. My goodness me, it was a maze. We got off at Kings Cross then had to change over to Paddington. From Paddington we went to Castle Cary and then we got a taxi to Laurel Lane, Queen Camel. I had always imagined what the English countryside looked like, but I have to say it was as though I had walked into a storybook village.

The centre was situated down a long, narrow lane with really quaint houses with thatched roofs and beautiful gardens. I was struck by the silence and peace in the whole place. Once we had booked in, we went along to the communal dining area and met some of the people who lived and worked there. My son introduced me and after we had eaten, he went for a walk and one of the members came and sat with me and we started to chat. She asked me how I felt about the place and if I had any questions.

I promptly replied, 'Well, actually, I just came to check you all out. I thought my son had joined a cult.'

She was taken aback at my answer, and I followed that up with, 'If you are truly spiritual, why do all the books talk about Christ Consciousness all the time? I don't see any books about Guru Nanak – *he* was a spiritual leader.'

Well, that was my mistake, right there. This lady took me by the hand and led me through to the library where there were books from all religions and faith beliefs, including the life of Guru Nanak. At the core of them all was the ethos that spirituality matters, regardless of the faith belief. I was truly humbled.

The next morning at breakfast, I was given smiles and nods by everyone. I think they had all heard about my outburst. I continued to go to the Centre whenever I could after that first visit. I found the peace, tranquillity and the meditation practices helped me so much in my quest for inner peace and answers to my loss. During this time I started reading many books relating to spirituality and that began to make sense to me, but I worried that I was getting 'above' myself by thinking I understood matters of the spirit.

I then read the book, *Autobiography of a Yogi,* and found myself on a path of self-realisation. Reading about spirituality from different perspectives made me revisit my Sikh Faith. It was this spiritual essence that held me together. Over the years we visited the centre many times and each time I came away with a better understanding of the difference between spiritual being and religious being. For me, it made me reconsider the Sikh scripture and unravel what was cultural and what was religious. It helped me to understand how our scriptures were there to guide us as individuals and not as a set of rules that were to be followed dogmatically, as prescribed by our learned male giannis.

*

Over the years I became more comfortable with myself as being spiritual rather than religious. It is a continuous journey that I am still undertaking. Although it has been tested many times, my faith is at the core of all that I do.

Our first visit and pilgrimage to India had been in 1988, which was an eye-opener and made me realise just how much we were considered outsiders back home. Every time I went back to India I returned home with more feelings about who, what and where I belonged. Others like me, the first generation born in the UK in the 50s, didn't really fit in in India because, although the connection was there mentally, we had a different way of thinking. But our attitudes were not completely 'white' either. I couldn't understand why we allowed ourselves to be so controlled by everyone, so many Indian women who were born in the UK had no life. Yes, I understood that we should be grateful for having a roof over our heads and food to eat, but what about the life force inside you? Why were we not allowed to feel that and see where it would have taken us?

6

Life After 1984

1984 truly was an 'annus horribilis', both for the Sikh people
worldwide and for us, the Singhs of Elm Row, Edinburgh. But
life goes on. So, my eldest daughter, Radha, was born in December
1984, Neelam arrived in 1986 and my youngest son, Dilal, in 1989.

In the wake of Rungu's death, I received immense moral support
from both my sisters and their families, along with John's brothers, my
brothers and their families and my lifelong friend, Sheila Dhariwal.
Without that support I would not have survived the emotional
rollercoaster that had become our life.

What I needed was someone to understand my internal turmoil
and see how tormented I was by living this life, caught between two
cultures. It was literally driving me mad. My health visitors were
lovely people but didn't understand my culture and couldn't help me
properly. They didn't know how to because we didn't communicate
meaningfully. It was then that it really hit me, that we Bhat women
were still an invisible community to society at large. We interacted
with the wider community to a limited extent, but withdrew into our
own 'invisible culture' as often and as quickly as we could.

I couldn't access the external support available because this was
not what we Bhat women did; we had our own ways of dealing with
bereavement and these, sadly, took no account of my feelings as an
individual. No-one, either in my own community or in the wider
Scottish society, understood my frustration of straddling two cultures.
The wider community in general regarded us Sikhs as a bright,

peaceful community – no-one recognised the hidden issues below the surface. The loss of my son made me realise that something had to change. We Bhat Sikh women could not go on as we were, always waiting for someone else to help us. I would look at my daughters and think, 'We have to stop doing this simply because it's accepted practice for us.' I'd wanted to do so much more with my life and didn't, because of these invisible barriers.

I began to recognise, and then to suggest, openly and publicly, that our situation was questionable. From there I identified (to my mind at least) the issue to be one of distorted cultural ideology. I learned more about my religion and about women and realised our treatment was not about religion, it was *cultural*.

Guru Nanak, the pioneer of Sikhism, promoted social equality between the sexes. I wanted to follow my faith, free of the cultural doctrines that had become so enmeshed in our way of life. Our families wanted us to distance ourselves from the influences of Western society because they thought this was the right thing to do, but there was no reasoning behind this attitude. Conversely, although it is important to make changes in life, I had no intention of abandoning my religious beliefs or important cultural traditions – my spiritual connection with the scriptures was far too deep for that.

Women of all ages in our community suffer injustices of multiple forms, yet most take the easy option. They say things like, 'Oh, that's the way it's always been.' Within marriages, the husband can go out and socialise but his wife is expected to stay at home, shut off from the outer world, and put a brave face on her situation, act normally even though there is no real relationship between husband and wife. She is expected to accept her situation of continuous unhappiness. Once a Bhat woman has married, she must do as her in-laws dictate, even though it is obvious that those same in-laws have separate rules for the daughter-in-law compared with their own daughters, who are treated much more leniently.

'Any act to change the world around us begins with us. It starts with a sense of agency, a sense that we have the power to effect change. The Latin root of the word "power" means "to be able".'[6]

At the time, I didn't know these words of Valarie Kaur's, but as time went on, I realised that 'when we feel helpless in the face of injustice, it's easy to give into the idea that this is just the way things are, because it's the only way things have been. Then someone comes along and sparks our imagination – a prophetic voice from the past or a friend on the phone.'[7] In my case it was both those things that were my trigger.

'We begin to see that the norms and institutions that order this world are not inevitable but constructed – and therefore can be changed. The Brazilian educator, Paulo Freire, calls this internal shift 'critical consciousness', the moment we tap into our own power to change the world around us.'[8] It feels like waking up. I could not see my own power but I knew I had to hold onto my conviction that I had to do something. I didn't know then that all my thoughts would be confirmed on my three year journey at university.

I wanted to use my life experiences to identify and highlight the invisible internal barriers that we faced which prevented us from moving forward, especially us Bhat women, but also women in the wider Sikh community. I wanted to create something that would empower, inspire and encourage the women from the Bhat community to claim the equality that was their right. And so the journey to create Sikh Sanjog began, in 1987.

---

6   *See No Stranger,* Valarie Kaur P76
7   *See No Stranger,* Valarie Kaur P76
8   *See No Stranger,* Valarie Kaur P76

7

Sikh Sanjog[9]

WHY SIKH SANJOG WAS FOUNDED: BEING A BHAT SIKH WOMAN IN SCOTLAND IN THE 20TH-21ST CENTURY

I realised that in order for me to get the help I needed, I had to open up to someone. In 1986-87 I became involved with Leith Home-Start, who provided a befriending service.

Home-Start was founded in Leicester, in 1973, by Margaret Harrison. She believed that supporting a family was best done in their home where the support can be shaped to the needs of the family. She realised that if parents got support and friendship from another parent, they would be better equipped to cope with life's many difficulties (post-natal depression, isolation, physical health problems, bereavement, to name but a few) and be able to give their children the best possible start in life. This movement rapidly spread across the UK and now 13,500 home-visiting volunteers support over 27,000 families and 56,000 children. Home-Start came to Leith in 1986.

Within my first year of contact with them, I was invited to join their board. I explained to them some of the internal cultural barriers and unspoken rules that we Bhat Sikh women faced: that I needed to have permission from my mother-in-law to go anywhere, even though

---

9   Sikh Sanjog means Sikh Links

I had been married for ten years and had two children; that going out on my own with my children was not acceptable – one went out as a family or not at all; that work and education were matters for the men, not us women, to decide; that socialising must always occur within community circles – we were never allowed to go out as a group of female friends.

As a member of the board of Leith Home-Start, I worked alongside a social work student who conducted a needs analysis for Sikh women in Leith. The paper she wrote concerning this work formed the basis of our first funding application to Edinburgh City Council, consequent upon which, in 1989, we started the Leith Sikh Community Groups. This organisation was founded by myself and other women from the Edinburgh Bhat Sikh community, as well as members of the wider Scottish community. The latter were people who believed in the vision we had and who were intrigued that they, as Scottish women, had lived alongside Sikh women without understanding the internal barriers they faced. For my part, I worked in the background for two years as advisor to the board of Leith Sikh Community Groups.

In 1991, I was asked to help develop the Edinburgh City Council's first Women into Work BME course, and was a participant on this course. This required me to do a 12 week placement which I did with Leith Sikh Community Groups. In the same year, I was offered the post of Outreach Worker, which I very hesitantly accepted as I had never worked in any capacity before. This made me the first Sikh woman from the Bhat community in Edinburgh to work outside a family business in a mainstream work environment.

THE EARLY YEARS OF SIKH SANJOG

The first few years were spent at 15 Smith's Place, in Room 6, having coffee mornings which doubled as Management Meetings. It took a long time for the Sikh women to see us as independent from Home-Start. The next ten years were spent making contact with, and gaining the confidence of, the women and the community as a whole, trying to persuade them to see us not as a threat but as a helping hand.

In 1999 we became a company Limited by Guarantee and changed our name to Sikh Sanjog. For me, its aim was to provide a secure environment in which women of the Edinburgh Sikh community could meet and take part in educational and recreational activities and gain new experiences. Its intent was to 'foster a positive sense of racial and cultural identity and involve members in the planning and organisation of the groups to promote confidence in their own abilities'. It has been my major life's work.

In addition to helping the women of the community to achieve their potential, I worked very hard over the years to gain the trust and respect of the male members of the community. Along the way I suffered considerable personal hurt at the disrespect and gender attitudes of some. But I persevered, with the result that now more and more Sikh men accept that equality for their daughters is important in their family life. They realise that education is important for both the boys and the girls of the community. I feel that, through my own achievements as a female member of the community, I have served as a role model to which the younger generation of Sikh girls can aspire.

What kept me going was the fact that there was no recognition whatsoever of the existence of our girls and women by people outside our community. If visitors from public bodies came to our Sikh Temple (which is also the community hub), they only ever met the men – which was not their fault, they were merely being culturally sensitive and wishing not to offend. In a strange way, my strength and perseverance came from my faith and the teachings of Sikhism, which promotes the equality of women with men in all walks of life. I was determined that people should acknowledge and recognise the women of our community, not treat us as if we were invisible.

Funding in the early years was easier to access than it is now, as we were one of a very small number of ethnic projects. Our core funding came from Edinburgh City Council and this source still forms a part of our funding. If I could go back in time, I think it would be to ensure that we were acknowledged more for the work we started, given more status within the City Council as service providers, rather than as a grant-funded Black Minority Ethnic organisation. But at the time I was simply glad that somebody was actually helping us. Over the past 35 years our projects have been very varied. The core work, namely the youth work and community development, has continued to receive funding from Edinburgh City Council, but in order to provide the other services and activities that we have adopted we have needed to fundraise thousands of pounds from alternative sources: Trusts, Foundations and Big Lottery. This is an ongoing issue which will probably never be resolved unless we become part of the service provision directly linked to the council.

In hindsight, I should have believed in myself and taken the post of Project Manager of Sikh Sanjog at the very outset, but I had no confidence in myself. The fact that I had left school at 13, was Sikh and had never worked anywhere in my life were personal barriers that I could not overcome at that time. I chose to stay in the background and took the title of Outreach Worker. Thus I became the backbone of the project without ever gaining recognition for all the work I was doing.

It was not until 2009 that I became aware of the meaning of 'covert' or subtle discrimination and patronising behaviour.

Unfortunately, when it hit home it shook me to my foundations. This was a huge learning curve for me and it made me look at what racism, discrimination, bullying and harassment can mean to an individual or a community. I had always assumed that I was Scottish Sikh, but others did not see me like that. They saw me as a Sikh woman from a 'backward community'. If I could turn the clock back, I would have taken the title of Project Manager then and been proud of who I was, would have allowed myself the pleasure of knowing that I had created a project that was (and is) providing a great service to the whole community.

But there were also times when I could see the funny side of things. For example, I would arrange a meeting with someone at Edinburgh City Council and, when I walked in dressed traditionally, I could see the person I was due to meet looking behind me for someone else. And when I opened my mouth and out popped this broad Glasgow accent, it was as if I had suddenly developed two heads! If only I had had a mobile phone then… I suppose, if I had taken every incident seriously, it could have led to many reports of discrimination. Even now, when I am the Director of the organisation, there will be occasions when someone will come in, looking for the 'chief', and look past me, expecting to see someone else. There is still an expectation that the Director will be white. Which is sad – we have been here for a long time and we now feel part of the Edinburgh community, yet that same community still regards us as 'other'.

At the Annual General Meeting of Leith Sikh Community Groups (we changed to Sikh Sanjog in 1999), held on 7 April 1992, Ashan Devi Bhaker (my older sister), then Chairperson of Leith Sikh Community Groups, made the following statement:

'The history of Leith Sikh Community Groups since the last AGM … has been one of change and often difficult change. However, without change there cannot be growth and development and it is our belief that Leith Sikh Community Groups is now considering some of the difficult issues in a constructive way and we hope that progress towards a secure future for the organisation is underway.'

Sikh Sanjog is the only organisation within the UK which aims to meet the needs of the Bhat Sikhs, specifically the women within that community. Ever since the inception of the project, the funding and resources provided to sustain it have been inadequate on all fronts: recreational, educational and social. The existing workload is demanding, a situation that is exacerbated by the fact that we are engaged in working in a specialised way with a specific culture that brings with it its own very unique demands. In particular, we work with women who are still not fully emancipated and in whom it is necessary to promote a positive sense of Sikh identity. And the demands of the project change constantly as we address the needs of second, third and fourth generations of Bhat Sikh women. We now work with girls and women from other ethnic minorities, too. The enormous benefits of this work are the breaking down of interracial and intercultural barriers, and the creation of a safe place for women to work together, enjoy each other's culture and learn about those common values that are shared by all women, irrespective of race, colour or creed.

No one can play a leading role in the running of an organisation for over thirty years, as I have, without a great deal of help and support from others. In my case, that help has come from a wide range of people – community workers, practice teachers, politicians, council workers, extraordinary colleagues and mentors. Over the years many changes have taken place. We now have a diverse group of board members and, without their understanding of the culture and needs of the women we serve, we would not be here today.

*

In February 2012 I was asked if I would become an Honorary Chaplain for Edinburgh University, following an initial approach by Ali Newell, the Assistant Chaplain. A little later, I met the chaplain, Harriet Harris, who had asked me for the names of four references and I provided these. I was really excited about this new function. It would be time-consuming, but I hoped it would result in the development of a new place of worship for Sikhs (and perhaps others) who were looking for a holistic spiritual place. One year later, as Honorary Sikh Chaplain to Edinburgh University, I managed to get together some Sikh students, including Satnaam Dosanjh and a Pakistani student, Zulfi (who was really interested in Guru Nanak's teachings) and together we created the first ever Sikh Student Association in Edinburgh University. The inception day of this association, the 21st November 2013, will go down in the Edinburgh University annals as an historic day (I think so...)

In my expanding portfolio of functions at this time, I was also encouraged to apply to the Community Development Standards Across Scotland Board. This was a bold initiative, coming initially from the Scottish Community Development Centre and strongly supported by Communities Scotland. It provided a way in to addressing longstanding issues such as no representation of BME groups on decision-making at board level and the lack of understanding of the lived experience of barriers which are faced by BME people in accessing mainstream services, but started from a fresh angle.

The Standards were developed with the involvement of both community organisations and agencies and were to apply to all partners in an engagement; but it was also clearly implicit that they could be seen as a tool for communities to hold agencies to account. When the Standards were launched in 2005 as a joint Scottish Executive/Convention of Scottish Local Authorities (CoSLA) document, endorsed by bodies including Scottish Enterprise, the

Scottish Council of Voluntary Organisations (SCVO) and the Association of Chief Police Officers in Scotland (ACPOS), this widespread support for a practical means of shifting influence to communities was a landmark. Things have moved on considerably since then and the organisation has changed and developed over the years, creating routes into Community Development training and a better understanding of the very diverse communities of Scotland.

I was involved with this work for about three years and then resigned. It was full of people who knew each other from local authority teams. Not that I was not welcomed, but after a while you realise that you're not in the right place. However, it was a learning curve for me and most of the time I made an impact by just asking what I deemed to be the 'obvious' questions, like why were there no other BME people on any of the other committees? I was also very surprised by the amount of money that was spent on away days and training days at very posh hotels. People would come and stay overnight to join the meetings in the morning and some were even flown down from London!

In January 2014, I was invited to give an address to the Scottish Parliament in a slot termed 'Time for Reflection'. This was an opportunity for external speakers from religious and other belief groups to share a message with the assembled politicians. I was there to represent the Scottish Sikh Community in my capacity as Founder/ Director of Sikh Sanjog. The following is the transcript of my speech:

'The purpose and function of Sikh Sanjog is to empower and inspire women of all ages and races to rise above internal and external discrimination that hinders their progress.

'We have developed and established a range of methods of connecting with women, encouraging them in their learning, creating practical opportunities to develop their skills and knowledge. Our aim is to close the inequalities gap, especially in terms of disadvantage and exclusion relating to education, skills, training and employment.

'Our ethos is based on the teachings of Sikhism. Guru Nanak Dev Ji, the founder of Sikhism taught that, in addition to the spiritual dimension, there is an important social dimension to the Sikh religion, focussing on social equality, rejection of caste discrimination and centrality of community service. The most revolutionary declaration of Sikhism in the 15th century was equality asserted to women. Essentially, Guru Nanak created an equal seat for everyone at the table, and an opportunity for dialogue where none existed. Guru Nanak embraced the entire human race. He said, "Recognise the divine light of God in each individual, treat all equally without prejudice of race, caste, religion, gender or social position."

'As Sikh Sanjog goes forward to celebrate its 25th anniversary this year, we continue to improve communication between professions and political parties of the needs of the Sikh and other BME women. The needs of Sikh women have changed over the last 25 years, but sadly, they have not gone away and, as within many disadvantaged groups, the women are further marginalised. Today the voices of women from within BME communities are still unheard. There is still discrimination of opportunity and barriers still hold them back from making an effective contribution to Scottish society. Most of the Sikhs living in the UK belong to families which have been established here for at least four generations; we are British citizens. We are taxpayers here. So we Sikhs in Scotland have a right to all that is available from the Scottish Government, its councils, NHS and other service providers, both as individuals and as organisations within our communities.

'As Guru Nanak inspires Sikhs to respect every individual, I see this reflected in the Scottish Parliament. Social Justice is a natural consequence of civic responsibility and reminds us that we cannot be insular.'

HIGHLIGHTS OF THE JOURNEY OF SIKH SANJOG

Case History 1

Sikh Sanjog obtained permission from Edinburgh City Council to have the very first Vaisakhi Parade in Edinburgh, in 2005. We took the letter of authorisation from the council to present it at the Gurdwara since the religious aspect would need the input of the gianni; furthermore, the whole community would need to be involved.

However, the Gurdwara committee were furious that we had dared to write to the council under the Sikh Sanjog banner instead of through the Guru Nanak Gurdwara committee. Indeed, they made a huge commotion about it and some felt that the parade should not go ahead because they had not been consulted about sending the letter to the council. Eventually, both to pacify the situation and because we were determined that the parade should go ahead, we agreed to remove the 'Sikh Sanjog' name completely from the application.

We told them that they could contact the council to get verification of the parade under the name of the Gurdwara. Following this rebuttal, the Board at Sikh Sanjog agreed that our tactics needed to change because we were clearly a problem that the Gurdwara Committee could not cope with. So we suggested to them that we would not operate under the banner of Sikh Sanjog Women's Group, but as Guru Nanak Gurdwara Ladies' Committee. This was agreed by all, with one exception. So, in preparation for the Vaisakhi Parade, seven of us met at the Gurdwara for four to five hours each day in the three weeks following the meeting with the Gurdwara committee, preparing items, making flags, organising food, etc.

But when it came to recognition as to who was doing what with regard to the parade, all accolades went to the men, with no mention of all the hard work the women of Sikh Sanjog had put in. The parade is now in its 17th year and it is only acknowledged by a very few that Sikh Sanjog were involved in the groundwork that went into making this event happen. This episode made me all the more determined to find a way to start up a new Gurdwara with a welfare centre attached to it.

Case History 2

In October 2007, the women's group went on a trip to Barcelona, the first time that a group of women from our Edinburgh Bhat Community had travelled abroad without any men in tow. So, we were the talk of community! We were now in our own premises at 22 Laurie Street, Leith, Edinburgh. From our humble beginnings in the kitchen of 15 Smith's Place, 17 years previously, we had moved into our own rented accommodation.

Punjabi Junction Social Enterprise Community café: the jewel in our crown

On the 1st of February, 2008, I started my new, redesigned job, moving from Outreach Worker to Business Manager/Outreach Worker for Sikh Sanjog's Punjab'n de Rasoi (Punjabi Women's Kitchen) Catering Project, a new venture which we had created within Sikh Sanjog. It was a great day for all the Bhat Sikh women of Edinburgh when we launched the pilot for our Social Enterprise Punjab'n de Rasoi café. We had rented space at the Acorn Centre Methodist Church in Junction Place for two days a week.

There were about 150 people at the opening, including councillors, funders and business people. We traded for seven months and then stopped to reassess. I was instructed by the manager to apply for funding if I wanted to take the Social Enterprise further. I had no knowledge or understanding about PR or marketing – it was a completely new world. I was thrown an application form to apply to the Scottish Government Third Sector Fund. This was the first application that Hilary Jones and I worked on and it was successful; we received a one-off start up grant of £70,000 to help establish the café.

During 2008-9, Hilary Jones (our current chairperson), and I obtained funding from five different funders, totalling over £280,000, together with a grant of £45,000 over three years. Not bad for someone who was baffled by application forms only two years previously!

At the beginning of 2008, I had been asked to give a short interview on the radio about how the Sikh Community in Edinburgh viewed the launch of the Scottish Sikh Heritage Trail in Edinburgh Castle. It had been very last minute but I had agreed to do it. On the 29th of September 2008, late Monday evening, I received a phone call from a PR person who was working on the promotion of this launch. He had been forwarded my name as a 'prominent' member of the Sikh community in Edinburgh. They wanted my views on what this meant to the Sikh community in Edinburgh. Scottish Minister for Culture, Linda Fabiani MSP, would be hosting an evening reception at Edinburgh Castle to launch the Scottish Sikh Heritage Trail on Tuesday 30th September.

They wanted me to come to Edinburgh Castle at 7 a.m. on the 30th to talk to them live on radio! I was annoyed at first, thinking, 'What a cheek, asking me at the last minute. How long have they known about this?'

My next thought was, 'What exactly does the Sikh Community think about having a Scottish Sikh Heritage Trail launched in Scotland?'

To be honest, I don't think many people, certainly the ones

within my own immediate and wider circle, were aware of the Sikh connections with the Raj, or for that matter the link with the Black Prince of Perthshire. However, there were others who were aware of these connections and the history behind it.

As for me, the thought of going to the castle at seven in the morning, especially when the weather was awful – it was pouring with rain at the time of the call and the forecast was the same for the next day. I said I would think about it and asked if they could call me back in half an hour. I told my husband and said, 'I'm not going. They want me there at seven in the morning. It's pouring with rain and anyway, I always get invited or called as the last resort!'

He said I was being daft and should just go – 'Tell them to get you a taxi, 'cause I'm not driving up there at that time in the morning.'

So I agreed to do the interview and a taxi picked me up at 6.45 a.m. When we arrived at the castle esplanade, it was blowing a gale and the rain was lashing down. They gave me a big brolly for cover and asked a few questions with regards to the launch. I said the first things that came into my head, 'Yes, the Sikh community of Edinburgh was very proud and looked forward to being part of the Scottish Heritage Trail in the future to see what it would uncover,' all the while thinking, 'It's freezing. I'm an idiot, standing here in the rain and half the Sikh community probably couldn't give a toss about this. They've probably got more pressing things going on. Furthermore, who's going to be listening to the radio at seven in the morning? The things I do – I must be mad!'

Well, I got home and there was an invitation from the organisers of the launch for me and my husband to attend the launch at the castle. Staff from Sikh Sanjog had also been invited. At the launch that evening I was tapped on the shoulder by a man who I had never met before, didn't know who he was. I was completely taken aback. He introduced himself as Mr. Jonathan Murray. He said he was the

124

one responsible for the PR and he just wanted to thank me for doing the interview at such short notice. If I ever needed any help with PR I was to call him. He was doing PR for the Scottish Government at that time also. This one encounter led to a heaven-sent link for Sikh Sanjog that would create amazing opportunities to connect with politicians and people we would never usually have had the chance to make contact with.

A year later I called Mr. Murray and asked for his advice and he came up trumps. I asked for his help in getting some high profile person to come and open our Social Enterprise Community café, Punjabi Junction, in March 2010. Through his links with the Scottish Government, he arranged for John Swinney, who was the Minister for Finance at that point, to come and officially open the café. I was advised by Jonathan that Mr. Swinney would be on a very tight schedule so he would basically be in and out. I have to admit I didn't know who Mr. Swinney was at that point. I just assumed he was some high heid yin from the Scottish Government and hadn't really asked Jonathan who he was or what he did.

I was just glad that we were actually on the verge of opening our very own Social Enterprise. It had been a tumultuous journey to get to this stage. Fraught with internal strife verging on discrimination, harassment and victimisation. I had suffered so much on a personal level that to get to this point was a feat in itself. So many of the women had volunteered their time, working into the night making curtains, setting tables, cooking, whilst still thinking, 'What will the community say? What will people think?' This was never far away from our thoughts.

So Mr. Swinney, and who he was, was not on my agenda in any way. On the morning of the 7th of March 2010 we had everything in place including all our Sikh ladies who had worked so hard and pushed their own internal boundaries to be a part of Bhat Sikh women making history! It was indeed just that: we were the first and only Social Enterprise in Scotland to be founded and run by Bhat Sikh women, and still are.

Mr. Swinney and his entourage arrived, led by Jonathan, who was signalling me to ensure that we kept to time and to just let him get on with opening the wee curtain that we had put in front of the plaque on the wall. (This had been made in India and brought over by my husband as it was too expensive to get done here!) Then he would leave. It occurred to me that I did not know how to address this man, so I kind of veered my way across to Jonathan and said, 'Who is he and what does he do?'

Jonathan whispered, 'He's the Finance Secretary for the Scottish Government,' and then it all clicked. We had received funding from the Scottish Government – £70,000 from the Scottish Government's Third Sector Enterprise Fund. This was funding that had been secured by myself and Hilary Jones, our board member. I don't think Mr. Swinney had ever met ordinary Asian women in this kind of setting so I really don't know what he was expecting. I do know that he stayed well over his time limit and actually went into the kitchen and had a go at rolling a chappati with a pinny on. Next day, the Herald had a pic with the caption 'Swinney in a pinny'.

He was amazed at the women all dressed in traditional clothes and that when they spoke their accents were Glaswegian, Brummie and Edinburgh. The women were very pleased with themselves, they had come so far that one of them actually said to him, 'If you had come to our place five years ago, we would not even have stayed in the same room as you. Whereas now we have gained so much from being part of Sikh Sanjog that we are sitting round a table having a chat with you.'

Below is a quote from the Leith Open Space Site:

'It's not just about women. Trishna lists the supporters who have helped turn a derelict property into a fresh and welcoming space with a gleaming modern kitchen. We are sitting on seats provided by Charan Gill (the Glasgow catering entrepreneur who featured in Channel 4's Secret Millionaire). Brian Smith of Dynamic Design Catering gave technical advice, Steve Cochrane of Dr Bell's provides ongoing guidance on customer care, David Court of McRae, Flett and Rennie gave legal advice and kept the fee low, and Jonathan Murray of Golley Slater PR ensures good press coverage.'

The café has been trading for ten years and we have attracted excellent PR and high profile visits:

In 2012 Madhur Jaffrey filmed an episode for her *Curry Nation* programme in the café and we have two recipes featured in her book *Curry Nation*.

In 2013 Paul Hollywood filmed an episode of *Pies and Puds*. He created Scottish Punjabi fusion fish pasties.

In 2013 Tony Singh and Cyrus Todiwala filmed an episode of *The Spicemen*.

We have been on BBC Radio Scotland's *Kitchen Café* and are currently recording for BBC Radio's new programme, *Curry Club*, promoting our Carrot Chutney.

We see ourselves as a bridge between the Sikh/Asian and Scottish communities. Food brings people together. We don't just look at our own community through this venture, we hope to create something which benefits the whole community. Our focus is on social mobility although social mobility shouldn't be judged by saying, 'Someone started at the bottom and got to the top.'

Social mobility should be about progressing, stage by stage, to the maximum of your potential, without ever having unreasonable or unfair barriers whether, as in the case of the women of our community, two main factors contribute to their disadvantaged position: external racism, emanating from the majority white community; and internal cultural pressures, which affect some of the minority ethnic women more than others.

Case History 3

On April 25th 2014 we celebrated the 25th anniversary of Sikh Sanjog at Edinburgh City Chambers. It was an amazing success at which Deirdre Brock, the Deputy Lord Provost of Edinburgh, and Sue King, the first worker at Sikh Sanjog, gave speeches. It was also the first time that Vasakhi has been acknowledged or celebrated in the City Chambers, another first for Sikh Sanjog.

Case History 4

In May 2014, a Scottish Referendum event was organised by Sikh Sanjog and CEMVO at the Leith Town Hall which was attended by Nicola Sturgeon, Deputy First Minister. This was the first and only pre-referendum event of its kind organised and hosted by the Bhat Sikh Community.

Case History 5

Sikh Sanjog has played a vital role in breaking down barriers, building bridges and planting the seeds of independence in Scotland's Sikh Youth.

One woman, Hardeep, started working for Sikh Sanjog as a Community Development Worker in 2010. I had convinced her that she had more to offer the world than simply enacting her roles as a mother and daughter-in-law. Hardeep had lived a traditional life, leaving school early and moving from her home in Birmingham to Scotland for an arranged marriage. When I met Hardeep, her fourth child had just started nursery and our meeting induced in her a life-changing moment. She now says, 'When I came into this organisation, I would say, "I have to do what I am told and not talk back," and Trishna would say, "Why do you have to do this? You can be independent, you can work, and at the same time you can still be a good daughter-in-law and a good wife."'

It is this recognition which Hardeep passes on to the children and young people that she now works with in Sikh Sanjog's weekly youth club. Both boys and girls, aged 5-16, can attend the club, where they are separated into relevant age groups. Hardeep says, 'Their imaginations are woken. They start thinking about what they can do in their lives.'

Hardeep felt this was particularly important for the predominantly Sikh members of the youth club, many of whom faced cultural barriers and a consequent struggle in navigating the differences between the Sikh and Western cultures. 'In Sikh culture, all the pressure comes for girls when they move into high school. At that age, they are predominantly working towards becoming a good daughter-in-law and a good wife. Parents will say to them, "You've got to learn how to cook," "You're old enough now, you've got to wear a traditional scarf," and "You don't go out playing with boys – that's a no-no." This juggling of two cultures creates all sorts of pressures; for example, when their friends are socialising in mixed-gender groups and they want to join them.'

Part of Sikh Sanjog's unique appeal is that its staff and volunteers have a firm understanding of both the culture and the religion of the Sikh community and, due to their work with women of all ages, are able to build bridges across generational divides.

'As a parent, I know how hard it is for mums,' Hardeep says. 'The parents are afraid that their daughter or son might run away, or fall in love with someone belonging to another culture: they feel that tradition has to be followed. So it's about understanding and speaking to the parents and saying: "It's okay, they're fine, you've just got to trust them a wee bit and talk to them."'

Generational disconnection can be even greater between grandparents and grandchildren, mostly caused by language barriers – the grandparents primarily speak Punjabi while the grandchildren can only speak English. To counteract this, Sikh Sanjog also supports grandparents though their health and wellbeing group. As Hardeep says, 'We gently introduce the idea that, if you really want to reconnect with and trust your grandchild – because it's the 21st century and you're still thinking phones are really bad – why don't you get WhatsApp or send emails or befriend them on Facebook?'

The importance of trust is a recurring theme. Much of the success of Sikh Sanjog's work hinges on the fact that families feel they can trust the organisation to have the best interests of their children, grandchildren and the wider community at heart. The organisation's connections to the Sikh community in Edinburgh are deep-rooted.

Hardeep again: 'For parents, Sikh Sanjog is a safe place for them to send their children. They're still being taught a wee bit about their culture and it's still about the Sikhism. We've got boys in the group as well and the parents are okay with that because it's a part of Sikh Sanjog.'

In contrast, many parents would be hesitant to send their children to another group. 'If they send them to someone else's organisation they might meet someone, they might make friends with a boy, and that's like losing their child in a way. But they know that here, because it's Sikh Sanjog, they're fine.'

Hardeep feels that the young people, too, share this trust in the Sikh Sanjog team, partly because of their awareness of the culture, and partly because they create an environment where their concerns and questions can be discussed openly. 'In my culture there's quite a lot of isolation – we're taught from a young age not to wash your dirty laundry in public, so you don't let anyone know you have a problem in your home. But that's changing now and that's why this organisation is here, so we try to get the kids to speak about it. They know this is a safe place.'

Vital to this process is creating opportunities for dialogue and education about the culture itself. 'We introduce the idea of choices and explain the difference between culture and religion, so if they have any queries about this we can help. People tend to mix the religion and the culture together and that's where the children get confused, thinking that it's our religion saying that we can't do this, or, we have to do that. The religion is totally different from the culture – culture is man-made, so you can add bits to and drop bits from it. Without us telling them, the young people realise that themselves as they come into the group and mature within it.'

The impact which this realisation has on the young people is transformative, Hardeep notes. 'Some of them were very shy when they first came in. They didn't talk to each other and now – they can talk! So much so, that sometimes you have to say, "Right, okay, let someone else speak now!"

'It's nice when you hear them talk about themselves saying things like, "I want to do this, I want to be that," because you're opening up choices for them. You watch their little faces light up. It doesn't matter if they're different, they can do what they want and the culture and the religion are not stopping them.'

The organisation also helps to break down barriers for Sikh children with learning disabilities, autism, or mental health issues. These are major issues in a culture in which such topics are still regarded as taboo. We provide a forum in which parents can come to us and say, one-to-one, 'Well, my child has autism, where do I go?' Such support can be a lifeline for parents whose own family may have let them down, and who may fear someone in the community finding out, due to the associated stigma. And the organisation/community relationship can and does work in reverse, so that a Sikh Sanjog worker who spots signs that a child has got learning difficulties can go to the parents and raise the matter with them.

Even the simple fact of seeing Sikh women working at Sikh Sanjog as Youth Workers, Development Workers, as the Director, sends a powerful message to the young people – and the parents – who step through the organisation's doors. As Hardeep says, 'It's all about putting choices in their heads. I have a daughter who is working, independent, who drives, has studied at college then university and has a Masters in English Literature and a degree in teaching. If I had never come to this organisation, I wouldn't have fought for my daughter to acquire these skills. Now, my favourite part of this job is watching when someone leaves the group, knowing that they're going to go into a career.'

Now, with over 30 years of service delivery, what started as a small meeting between a few women has grown into a robust organisation, offering a range of pro-active solutions helping women to feel comfortable in themselves and accomplish their goals: developing employability skills, progressive therapy and youth programs.

I think this speech given by the Lord Provost, Frank Ross, on the night of our 30th Anniversary celebrations hosted by Edinburgh City Council, at the City Chambers, summed it all up:

'I am delighted to be here today, on behalf of the citizens of this great and historic city, to welcome you all to the beating heart of civic Edinburgh, here in the City Chambers to celebrate the work and achievements of Sikh Sanjog which has operated since 1989.

Reaching 30 years of continual operations is a key milestone for any organisation, but for a community project to have grown so substantially, from relatively humble beginnings, and which services the needs of highly vulnerable minority ethnic girls and women, is a remarkable accomplishment, and one which those involved, both past and present, should be rightly highly proud. While Edinburgh is an inclusive city, is a diverse city, is a city of partnership, is a city of engagement that puts our citizens at the heart of what we do, it remains the case that, against the backdrop of a successful economy and substantial employment, around 30% of residents continue to experience profound poverty and disadvantage.

In a city which is a top-20 EU visitor destination, and ranked number one in the world for liveability, it remains a concern that so many of our fellow citizens experience substantial challenges in their lives which prevent their attaining their outcomes. For some specific groups of residents, additional barriers can exist, which require bespoke and sometimes intensive assistance in order to help deliver personal potential. Sikh Sanjog has done just that over the last three decades, building a positive and purposeful city-wide (and national) reputation for shaping support primarily around the needs of individual girls and women of Bhat Sikh and minority ethnic heritage. Over the years their services have extended to women from all ethnic and Scottish communities, unlocking potential and transforming lives.

I understand that Sanjog means 'linking' in the Punjabi language, and demonstrates the core objectives of the organisation to be a bridge for: understanding and engaging with Scottish Society, assessing education and career possibilities, accessing one-to-one counselling services, and continued bespoke support to open up new opportunities and potential.

In a complex city, a level of personal confidence and educational attainment are key to unlocking better life-chances, which can be transformative across generations. Sikh Sanjog's efforts to unleash the personal potential for their clients, and their working in partnership with the city's public, business, and third sectors, has helped deliver increased volumes of bespoke youth provision, high-skilled employment, and degree and post-graduate learning for minority ethnic girls and women across Edinburgh. Again, this is a substantial, and life-affirming contribution to our communities and one which is opening doors that were previously closed for the new generation of minority ethnic girls.

Alongside these achievements, as part of the City's long-held sustainability agenda, and allied to the Scottish Government's drive to grow social and community enterprise, in 2010 the Board installed Scotland's first minority ethnic women's social enterprise – The Punjabi Junction. At the time, this was ground-breaking, and even unheard of across Scotland. The café continues to provide traditional Punjabi home-cooked cuisine to the people of Edinburgh. The initiative also gives minority ethnic women training and employment opportunities, whilst learning valuable social and practical skills, improving their literacy, numeracy, communication, social and customer care skills, which are transferable and can readily be applied in the workplace. An additional benefit is that the women are interacting with people from all cultures. The Junction is now a cornerstone of Scotland's leading centre for growing ethical trading, where over 230 social enterprises successfully operate in a range of markets in our city.

If that wasn't enough, the café now operates an outside catering function, which has proven to be a huge success, with a range of corporate and occasion bookings. Many across the city, and many international visitors, as well as myself, will have noted with fondness, the delicious morsels made available as part of our flagship Edinburgh Mela festival of world music and dance.

Sikh Sanjog and its enterprises are a blueprint for how community spirit and determination can grow from a seedling, to stand tall and proud, in making a substantial and tangible difference to the lives and life-outcomes for those most vulnerable in our diverse society.

In closing, on behalf of the citizens of Edinburgh, and the City of Edinburgh Council, I would wish to congratulate all of those involved, the Board, the staff, the volunteers, the partners and most of all, my sincerest congratulations to those of you who have made use of the project and maintained an involvement in order to put something back.'

8

By Royal Appointment

My first invitation from the Royal family came in May 1997. It was the 50th Anniversary Celebrations of the Commonwealth. I had come into the office on a cold, sunny morning in February and I sat at my desk and looked at all the mail. Something caught my eye – an envelope with what looked like a Royal embossed postmark. I sat, whirling around in my office chair, and opened the letter. When I read it, I was a bit bemused and then started to laugh, thinking, 'Which one of my six siblings is playing a prank on me?'

I read the letter a couple of times and then I started to call my siblings. They all thought I was nuts! Calling them at nine in the morning, asking who had sent me an invitation to the Palace. I reread the letter and was still not sure what to think. I waited until the other staff came in and then showed them the letter. They were also surprised, but pleased for me. I, however, was still puzzling over how I got this invitation. Me, a wee lassie fae Glesga, of immigrant parents. Who would invite me to St James's Palace? It must be a joke.

I took the letter home and my husband read it over, and although he was very pleased, with a slight smirk he said, 'Well, it's only you that's been invited.'

I thought, 'How can I go on my own? What will my mother-in-law say? In fact, what will anybody related to me say, as well as the whole community?'

That's how it was then: my thinking was always overshadowed by worries about what people would say. It was inherent in all the women I knew, that first initial thought. There was never that delight or instant self-satisfaction, always the wee niggle at the back of our minds. In fact, it wasn't at the back, it was always at the front. Everything else took second place.

So I thought about it and then reread the letter. It was just for me, but my husband was genuinely pleased for me and started planning the trip to London. His sister lived there so we could stay with her and he would accompany me to the palace gates and come back and meet me afterwards.

I still couldn't get it into my head that I would be going into the palace on my own. So I wrote a letter to the palace, explaining my situation, that as an Asian woman our culture did not permit us to go anywhere on our own, let alone visit the palace. Therefore, was it possible for my husband to accompany me? They replied very politely, saying NO, the invitation was for me in light of my work within the community and basically I could come or decline the invitation.

In the end we went and it was a most wonderful experience. I actually ended up pushing my way through a wee throng of people and shook hands with Prince Charles, all the while just looking at his jacket lapels and thinking, 'Gosh, for a prince, his suit looks well worn!' The other most wonderful thing was that my eldest brother, Gurdev, who worked in Glasgow, had also been invited in recognition of his community work, and so there we were, brother and sister at the palace. Who would have believed it? My husband and his sister came to meet me afterwards and we had our pictures taken with the Palace Guards. They were so tall, we looked like dwarfs next to them.

Then an invitation came from Sir Tom Farmer. The Royal Yacht, Britannia, launched at John Brown's shipyard, Clydebank, on April 16th 1953, was coming home to Scotland and being brought to her new home in Leith, following a fiercely fought competition in which the Forth Ports bid was successful, in 1998. Sir Tom had bid in the auction to secure the right to hold the first function on the Britannia. It was Sir Tom's wish that the people of Leith should be the first to be welcomed on board this historic vessel.

The Inaugural Reception took place on the yacht on the 11th of October 1998. It was such a wonderful evening – we were piped on board by the Pipes and Drums of the Argyll and Sutherland Highlanders. My husband was in his element, meeting Sir Tom and letting him know that he too was a proud Leither and a lifelong Hibs fan, and – after a few drinks – quoting his favourite phrase, 'We're a' Jock Tamson's bairns' to him. It made Johnny's night!

*

A year or so had passed since my visit to St James's Palace and I was thinking, 'The Royals visit other charities. Perhaps I should return the favour of being invited to St James's Palace and invite Prince Charles to come visit Sikh Sanjog in Edinburgh.'

Everyone at the office thought I was punching above my weight. They thought I was nuts, which made me even more determined. So I wrote to the Palace, inviting Prince Charles. The Palace took over a year to respond. They were apologetic and said that due to Prince Charles' very busy diary, he would not be able to visit Sikh Sanjog.

But then I was invited to the Garden Party at The Palace of Holyroodhouse in July 2002. This invitation was just for me – not Johnny. Again, my immediate response was to feel guilty, jaunting about on my own with Royalty. What would people say this time? Johnny was perfectly fine with it, and not at all bothered about the community's attitude. I think by this time he'd come to terms with the fact that my life was moving in a different direction to that of other women in the community. It was me who was constantly anxious about being judged for gallivanting around on my own, mixing with white men and women. Johnny was proud of me – he said, 'Just go. I'm fine with it, don't worry about what others say. No one's going to say anything to your face anyhow, they all just talk behind our backs.'

So, on a warm, sunny day in July 2002, I set off to Holyrood Palace. There were people queuing right along Holyrood Park to get in. Once inside the gardens, we were just in such a daze – were we actually here? The two staff members with me were both white Scottish women, and neither of them had even been inside Holyrood Palace before, let alone been invited to a Garden Party. This was the year that Prince Charles and Camilla had 'come out'. I got caught up with everyone clambering to squeeze in and shake hands with Prince Charles and Prince William, but to my annoyance, I ended up shaking hands with Camilla. And me a die-hard Diana fan! I remember thinking, 'Gosh, she's not much taller than me,' and feeling like I had somehow tarnished Diana's memory by shaking hands with the 'other woman'. Not that it would have mattered to either of them, obviously.

A decade later, to my great surprise, my big sister nominated me for the Charity (or Sewa – 'selfless service') category in the 2012 Sikh Awards. These annual awards have nominees from all over the world and, to my shock, I was shortlisted to the last three.

I saved up and booked train tickets and hotel rooms for all my family. The awards ceremony took place in the Park Plaza Hotel, London, which coincided with my 59th birthday. We had a lovely time! My youngest brother and both my sisters came, together with my four children, two grandchildren and my husband. My birthday was celebrated in style, starting with a facial and massage at the Hilton, courtesy of my brother. It was truly eye-opening, seeing how the other half live. The evening sky was bright with stars as we took taxis to the Park Plaza; I felt I could touch the moon. Doormen in top hats and tails opened the taxi doors, inside the tables were all set up with dinner stands and Oscar-style lamps in the centrepiece. I was only mildly disappointed when I didn't win the award – after all, I'd made the last three, me, the wee girl from Glasgow! It felt surreal, as if it was happening to someone else.

My youngest brother, Chander, organised a birthday drink after the awards in the Park Plaza Hotel, and my wee brother had put up birthday banners in the hotel's bar lounge with my name on them. He also asked a trombone player, a member of the resident band, to play *Happy Birthday* to me. Then they brought out the birthday cake.

*

On a really nice sunny day in May 2014, I went downstairs and picked up the mail. There was a letter there from the Cabinet Office, addressed to me. When I opened and read it, I couldn't believe my eyes. I went into the kitchen where my husband was and told him the letter was from the Prime Minister, informing me that I had been nominated for an OBE. His expression didn't change.

He just said, 'Oh, that's good. I did say to you a few weeks ago that someone will probably nominate you.' And he then gave me a kiss on the forehead and said, 'Right, I'll see you later, I'm going to the football match.'

I really needed to tell someone, so I phoned my daughter-in-law, Sharon, but I read the letter again and again and it said it was strictly confidential, so I told her not to say anything to my son or anybody else. She came round with a box of chocolates.

I told no-one else about the OBE since there were instructions in the letter stating that disclosure of the award to anyone else *had* to wait until June 14th , when the list would be made official.

I did phone Mary McKenna, who was our chairperson then, because I am sure she was the one who nominated me, but she was adamant that I should not mention the award offer to anyone, even her; she said that if knowledge of the award got out before the list was published they could remove your name from the list. We only spoke about it in a roundabout way, which made me laugh. The Queen's Birthday Honours List was finally released on Friday, 13th June, and I was on it. Me, Trishna Devi Pall Singh of Glasgow, had been awarded an OBE!

We had hosted an Akhand Path for Sikh Sanjog's 25th Anniversary in May 2014 and all sorts of people, having seen my name on the Honours list, were phoning and texting me, which was really exhilarating.

But when I went to the Gurdwara and started doing seva, I didn't mention my OBE to anyone. The police recruitment people had a stall at the Gurdwara, alongside the RAF, and we too had our own exhibitions and murals on display. I got talking to the police recruiter and told him I had been awarded an OBE. He was really impressed and pleased for me and asked me if I had told anyone. I said, 'No,' so he went outside to the kitchen and told everybody that I had been awarded an OBE and everybody came through and started kissing and hugging me. I had invited all our Sikh Sanjog Board members (Mary McKenna, Sarah Paterson, Sheena Ramsay and Hilary Jones) down to the Gurdwara so that we could present them with a saropa, which is a very prestigious honour within Sikhism, to thank them for their support over the years.

For my OBE investiture, we (my husband, four children, three grandchildren, daughter-in-law and myself) booked into the Holiday Inn at Bloomsbury Kings Cross. We left by taxi at 9.30 for Buckingham Palace, my husband telling the taxi-driver, 'We're going to get an OBE!'

We entered the palace by the South East Gate, the one that directly faces the famous balcony that the Royals stand on during all big occasions. All I could think was, 'Oh my God, Princess Diana stood on that balcony when she got married.'

We were taken through the main gates, past the guards (who were actually changing at that point), to the quadrangle where a horse-drawn carriage arrived with the Beefeaters, all in their red uniforms.

A Chelsea Pensioner welcomed us at the palace entrance and he asked, 'Who is the recipient?' Johnny nodded towards me, at which point the man moved my husband to one side and said to me, 'Madam, go through the hall towards the Grand Staircase, guests to the left, recipients to the right.'

The place was just unbelievable, it was so grand. There were huge vases on the floor, massive portraits on the walls, and full-liveried guards standing as still as statues. The staircase up to the Green Room was garlanded with so many Christmas decorations, I mumbled to myself, 'Oh my God.' The man at the top of the stairs must have heard me because he looked down and said, 'Madam, take your time.'

There were 94 people at this particular investiture. We were taken into a massive room with amazing pieces of furniture and artefacts; the settees were in gold and pink brocade or silk, which matched my outfit! We were given our instructions by a tall, uniformed man who talked us through the procedure. We were to walk forward to a lady who would check our name, then move forward to another uniformed man. When we heard our surname, and only then, we were to move forward to face Prince Charles, curtsy and walk towards him. Once at the podium we were to stop, he would pin on the medal, then speak to us. We were to address him as 'Sir' or 'Your Royal Highness'. Once he put his hand out to shake, that was the signal to end any conversation, walk backwards, curtsy and walk towards the other end of the Grand Ballroom where people were waiting to take the medal back, box it up and bring us back into the ballroom to be seated with all the guests.

The ceremony took place in the Grand Ballroom. Prince Charles was on a dais with two thrones behind him. On either side of him were two Beefeaters, stewards and the Lord High Chamberlain, who read out the names of the recipients.

The room had a balcony upon which there was a live orchestra playing. When I heard my name, I moved forward and Prince Charles asked me, 'Are there many Sikhs in Scotland?' to which I think I said, 'Yes, there are quite a number of us.' He then said, 'How many Gurdwaras are there in Scotland?' and I said, 'There are four in Glasgow, one in Edinburgh.' I can't exactly remember what he said after that, but I do remember saying, 'You must come and visit us,' to which he replied something like, 'I am sure I must.'

I came away and sat down in the ballroom, feeling strange about the whole thing. My thoughts were, 'My God, I am in Buckingham Palace. I've only ever seen pictures of the outside, I am actually inside now.' It's a totally different world and it confirms my belief of how our destinies are shaped and written before we are born. To see the palace was to see another world.

In the Green Room, I spoke to three people: two women, both English, both awarded MBEs. One was a Youth Worker who worked with young people in gangs and the other worked for the Department of Work and Pensions, specifically helping the homeless. The third person, a man receiving an OBE, was in the army and had worked in Kazakhstan. These people, like me, were amazed and awestruck by the splendour of the palace and the fact that they had been nominated for, and awarded, an honour.

Afterwards, in the Palace Quadrangle, we had family pictures taken by the official palace photographer. Then we climbed the steps of the big statue that stands opposite the main door of the palace and took some more pictures, then took taxis to Orso in Covent Garden for lunch. The staff there were really pleasant; they loved the colour we brought to the place and asked if they could take a picture of us to put on their wall! When the meal was over, they brought out a wee glass bowl with ice-cream and a sparkly candle to celebrate my OBE. After this, we all walked to Convent Garden, went into the National Portrait Gallery, then onto Leicester Square where we stayed until about 7 pm.

We had been invited to dinner that night at my husband's sister's place. We took the OBE with us and, I have to say, they were all so pleased and proud of the fact that someone from the Bhat community had achieved this honour. Their mother even said, 'You have done the Bhat community proud, your parents would be so proud of you.' They all had pictures taken with the OBE, with my husband holding it as if he was the recipient!

*

The Glasgow Gurdwara, which opened in April 2014, organised, for the first time in Scotland, a Scottish Sikh Achievement Awards ceremony, to recognise the achievements of Sikhs in Scotland. The event was held on the 30th of November 2014 at the Marriott Hotel, Argyle Street. I was invited as Guest of Honour in recognition of the fact that I was the first Sikh woman in Scotland to have been awarded an OBE. Before leaving for Glasgow, I got to thinking of how my forebears would have felt about my award and the recognition accorded me within the Sikh community. They would be so proud, I'm sure, especially my grandad and dad. This was the kind of work that they believed in, always helping the community. My mum would also have been happy for me, but in a different way; she disapproved of women being in the limelight in any way. That was for the 'open' women of the Sikh community – not Bhat women. But for me, it's always been, why not the Bhat women? And this event in Glasgow was all about the Bhat women, about us being recognized as trailblazers and equals.

My whole family accompanied me to Glasgow, together with 20 women from Sikh Sanjog. Strangely, there weren't many present there from the Bhat community, only eight from Glasgow and 30 from Edinburgh, which confirmed my feelings that there is something inherent in our community that makes it difficult for them to connect with others who are moving on in the world.

*

In January 2015, we were invited to dinner by the Chancellor of Edinburgh University, Lord Timothy O'Shea, at his residence in Heriot Row, in the New Town in Edinburgh. The place was amazing and comprised of four floors. A huge piano stood in the hall, which had two big pillars in the form of an archway and was the size of my study. Original paintings covered the walls. A butler and a maid served the food and drink. The Chancellor said that each house in the street was different. They had been designed and built for different professionals, particularly doctors or judges.

Four other people with partners had also been invited, all university people, professors and doctors, who had also received an OBE or MBE and were linked to Edinburgh University in some way. I felt very much out of place when the conversation turned to reminiscences about the old days at university when they were young. It's moments like these when it really hits home as to how much we Bhat women were denied in the name of 'our culture' and 'our community'. But that evening at the Chancellor's residence was an amazing experience and I went so far as to invite the Chancellor to visit Sikh Sanjog. In truth, he invited himself by asking about the Sikh Community in Edinburgh and by mentioning that he had visited a Gurdwara in London a few years previously. He also told me he went to India on a regular basis because the universities at Edinburgh and Delhi have strong connections.

*

In February 2015, in a complete departure from my normal activities, I went flying at RAF Leuchars in a Grob Tutor plane! This was arranged by Sarah Lockhart, our RAF contact, and Khaleda Noon (our then youth work manager) and I were picked up at 7 a.m. and driven to Leuchars by a very nice RAF man. We arrived in Leuchars about 8.45 a.m. and it was just like those RAF bases you see in old films, with barriers, checkpoints, people saluting, green buildings, the odd plane sitting beside big army trucks.

Once they had frightened the wits out of us with the demonstration DVD and simulator on how to jump out of the plane if anything goes wrong, we were taken away to be kitted out in overalls, polo neck, long johns, big thick socks and black boots. I didn't think I would fit into them all but I did! Then it was on with the parachute, lifejacket, helmet, sunglasses and white gloves. I actually looked really cool, even if I say so myself.

It was a beautiful clear day but we had to wait for take-off until they had clearance from the one and only police checkpoint in the whole of the UK, that our security check had been passed. It was a two-seater plane but I didn't feel at all scared or nervous. We flew over St. Andrews, Dundee and Crail; to the north, we could see mountains covered with snow. During the 30 minute flight, the pilot asked me if I wanted to steer or do a loop, but I declined both options.

*

In April 2018, I was contacted by Sarah Parker, the Inclusion Manager for the Royal Collection Trust, St James's Palace, London. Their research had shown that only a certain type of person visited places like the palaces and the Queens Gallery – uptake from the BME communities, disabled people and those living in deprived areas was minimal. So Sarah had the job of creating links with under-represented community groups across the UK.

I had been introduced to Sarah by the late Mr. Harbinder Singh, the Honorary Director of The Anglo Sikh Heritage Trail which has been running successfully in England since 2004, exploring the key locations in the capital linked to the heritage and culture of Sikhs and their relationship with Britain.

In 2008 Mr. Singh felt it was a natural progression to extend it to Scotland. Scotland has a long-established Sikh community, beginning with colonial India. It was an extraordinary experience. As I have detailed earlier in the book, we had a guided tour of the castle and saw the Honours of Scotland on display in the Crown Room for the first time. Although I had lived in Edinburgh for over 40 years and my husband lived here all his life, this was something that people from ethnic communities just didn't do. This was a white man's domain and although we were proud of our Scottish heritage we didn't see anything that linked us with this history until now. Learning about the links between Scotland and Sikhs was extraordinary.

So when Sarah Parker contacted me all those years later, with the opportunity of working with the Palace outreach team, I was thrilled. Sikh Sanjog had come such a long way, and what transpired from those meetings was even more amazing. We were introduced to the team at Holyrood Palace and asked to collaborate on developing and delivering workshops for the opening of the Splendours of the Sub Continent exhibition. Here we were, the once-invisible women of the Bhat Sikh community, leading workshops at a private viewing and talk at the Queen's Gallery in Holyrood Palace.

Giving the talk was Tony Singh, the famous Edinburgh-born Sikh chef, who also happens to be one of my nephews. It was surreal – at the end of the evening I asked Tony for a lift home, and as we were leaving the palace, the gates were opened for us. I turned to Tony and said, 'Would you have ever thought that we, aunt and nephew, would be leaving Holyrood Palace together and someone opening the gates for us?' and we laughed our heads off.

Over the next few weeks we received further invitations: a community visit and tour of the Holyrood Palace state apartments; a request to provide cultural awareness training to Holyrood Palace staff, and then – in 2019 – training sessions for staff at Windsor Castle and the Queen's Gallery in London. So off I went to deliver my humble, straightforward Sikh Cultural Awareness sessions. Buckingham Palace was a completely different experience to my last visit: this time I was issued with a dress code and taken through the staff entrance. Sarah walked me through the passageways and pointed out the amazing array of artefacts and paintings on display in each lobby or hallway we passed through. She pointed out the footman's corridor and the built-in wardrobes along the wall which were as high as the ceiling. These, she said, were for staff uniforms. We went for lunch in the staff dining room and as a lady with her tray passed by, Sarah whispered in my ear, 'She's one of the Queen's ladies-in-waiting!'

I delivered four sessions, over two days, to 60 staff. The first session was delivered in the training room of the Queen's Gallery and I was allowed to have a picture taken. The second day, we had a room actually inside the palace: there were paintings of Queen Victoria on the walls, huge chandeliers hanging from the ceiling and display cabinets full of china from around the world. During the breaks we had tea in cups with 'ER' on the bottom and water in bottles with 'ER' on them. I was told that no photography was allowed in this room, but I was allowed to take an empty water bottle home, and it is on display in the Welsh dresser in my kitchen. It was an eye-opening experience for me – the staff were nearly all from London, but knew surprisingly little about Sikh culture, or the history of how we had arrived on these shores, or what contributions the Sikh community had made to the country. As the discussion opened up, it was clear that most people had a positive impression – that Sikhs are friendly, keep themselves to themselves, wear turbans, and are very hospitable, colourful and successful – but had no idea of the real problems and internal barriers that Sikh women continue to face. Having the chance to explain and discuss these issues with the people who run the royal palaces, by telling them my own story, was amazing. And by all accounts our workshops and training sessions were a huge success: Sarah later said that it gave the Royal Collection the confidence to offer further sessions exploring other faiths, and to keep breaking down cultural barriers.

This partnership with Holyrood and Buckingham Palace led to our most recent hosting of a visit during the pandemic, in May 2021, of the Duke and Duchess of Cambridge. However, it was not solely due to that, it helped that we were known to people within the palace. One of my neighbours, George Fyvie, worked at the palace and had been involved in a meeting where the discussion had been around finding a replacement visit to a local charity for the Duke and Duchess. The original intention of going to Glasgow had been cancelled due to coronavirus restrictions. George knew about Sikh Sanjog/Punjabi Junction through the newly-created WhatsApp group for Craigentinny, where I posted info about what was going on. So he had mentioned the work we were doing with local food banks. This was very last minute and we were contacted by the Duke's private secretary to ask if the Duke and Duchess could visit our Punjabi Junction Café. We explained that although we were still working alongside local food banks, providing currys and chapattis, we did not have our own premises. Due to funding cuts and redevelopment of the Leith Walk area, we had not renewed our lease. We were so shocked at the request but quickly pulled ourselves together and came up with a plan and made a few suggestions. Ultimately it was agreed that Sikh Sanjog/Punjabi Junction – myself and five members of our staff: Jasbir Singh, Sinita Potiwal, Balvinder Singh, Satnam Singh and Darshan Kaur – would cook up a storm at the Queen's Gallery Café kitchen at Holyrood Palace, with the Duke and Duchess helping to cook and pack the containers that would be distributed to people who were receiving these food parcels. It was amazing to think that here we were, six women from the Bhat community, organising and hosting such an historic visit.

When I think about it now and compare it to what it was like for our women 35 years ago, I know we have truly changed the lives of so many women. The newspapers had a field day. Vogue Magazine India wrote:

'After Meghan Markle and Prince Harry showed support by setting up a fundraiser for COVID-19 relief efforts in the country, Kate Middleton and Prince William too came together yesterday with Scotland-based Sikh family support charity, Sikh Sanjog, to help the group prepare hot curry meals for disadvantaged communities in Edinburgh. In case you missed it, the Duke and Duchess of Cambridge are currently on a royal visit to Scotland, and the meeting with Sikh Sanjog saw the duo being guided by women from the organisation to whip up chapatis and curry at the kitchen in the Palace of Holyroodhouse, the Queen's royal residence in Edinburgh.

Snippets from the royal couple's Indian cooking session were also shared on their official social media channels, and an Instagram post showed both Kate and William enjoying the cooking process and interacting with the members of the community while trying their hands at turning out perfectly round rotis. When it came to seasoning the curry, Kate revealed that she does enjoy curries at home from time to time, saying, 'Yes, I love it.' To which the Duke added, 'She likes a bit of spice,' while also revealing that he himself is 'not too good with spice.' It may just have been another visit for the Royals but it was an amazing achievement for the women of the Bhat community.

9

Cap and Gown

Sometime in mid-2004, I was checking emails at work when something popped up with information about a new initiative between Glasgow University and an organisation called Linked Work and Training Trust. They were looking for applications from ethnic minority people who were working in the voluntary sector and had no qualifications. The course on offer was a BA in Community Learning and Development over three years – and in order to apply you needed to be working within a voluntary sector organisation, and have approval from your line manager and Board.

Well! I just stared at the screen and thought, I'm going to do this. My dream of going to university and wearing one of those hats at graduation was about to come true! I looked at the email and then read it a few more times. And then I began to understand what it would – could – mean to me.

All my life, growing up in Glasgow, I'd visit the Botanical Gardens and walk past the university, always wondering, how do people get in there? Why can't I be one of them? What is it like to be a student and have fun? Sadly, the culture was against me, and these were thoughts and dreams that no one ever heard. As a teenager, those possibilities were all in my head, but time and life moved on.

Now, suddenly, here I was, at the age of 51, with the opportunity of a lifetime staring back at me from my computer screen! I thought about it for a few seconds and then decided I was going to do this. I would go to university.

First, I spoke to the then manager of Sikh Sanjog and asked her opinion. At that time I was working part-time, two days a week, though it seemed like a full-time job as I was always on call, and women would phone me at home at all times. She agreed that I could work one day in the office and the other day would be for study time.

I really didn't know anything about office politics – I didn't even understand the concept. I just assumed everyone was as straightforward as they came across to me. I had no hidden agenda, or ambitions to take over Sikh Sanjog. In fact, I had no idea that having a degree would instantly raise my status, financially or otherwise. You may find this hard to believe, but it's the truth. I just wanted to go to university; just getting onto the course would be my dream come true.

There was obviously the application process to consider, and then the question of how I would manage my time between work, family and university coursework. But none of those things worried me at that time. All I wanted was for someone to say yes, go ahead. Johnny initially thought I was nuts, but supported my decision on the understanding that I would make sure everything at home continued as usual.

At the time, my eldest son, Rajvinder, and his wife, Sharon, had two children, Jeevan and Amahn, and they had moved into their own home the year before. My daughter, Radha, was engaged and the wedding was set for 2006. Neelam, my second daughter, was also engaged, with the wedding set for 2007. Dilal, my youngest, was 14 and still at school. So it was my call to decide how it was all going to work.

I had always believed in the words that came from the scriptures, that to oppress is wrong, but to remain oppressed and not challenge it is even worse. In some ways that had been a mantra throughout my life, always there in the back of my mind. And the words of Mahatma

Gandhi – you must be the change you want to see in the world – resonated within me as I looked back at that girl from Glasgow who had left school at 13 with no leaving certificate, no grades, just an angry passion to one day do something. I'd come such a long way. I had battled internally and externally, and arrived at this point in my life.

So I applied, and a few weeks later was invited to Glasgow for an interview with the tutors, Colin Duffy and Akwugo Emejulu. Colin was white Scottish, and Akwugo, who we called AK, was African American. I clarify this as it would have a profound effect on me as the course got underway. I was asked the – I presumed – routine questions that are asked of applicants, one of which was, 'Why do you want to take this degree?'

I replied perfectly honestly, asking them, 'Do you still get the mortarboard hat when you graduate?'

They said, 'Yes, why?'

My answer was, 'I just want to throw it up in the air when I graduate!'

They looked at each other, probably thinking I was completely mad, but just smiled and said they'd be in touch.

That year Johnny and I had planned a five-week trip to India with Radha, Neelam and Dilal: this would be their first visit to India. We were leaving in mid-October and returning in November. Obviously, I had no idea about semesters and when they started or finished. So we continued our planning, and then I received my acceptance letter, informing me that the course would commence in November. I was worried I'd lose my place, but after discussing with the tutors, I was allowed to miss the first sessions and join in January 2005.

Our trip to India was amazing. We came back absolutely knackered, but I was buzzing with excitement and worry about how my life was going be affected by university. I decided that each week I'd go to work in the office on Mondays, then Tuesday would be my day for university, Wednesday would be study and the rest of the week I would be catching up with housework and resting. Simple! But there are times in your life when you just can't plan in advance, and this was mine.

I did go into the office on the Monday, and on the Tuesday I left the house at 7 a.m. Johnny dropped me off at St Andrew's Bus Station, and I caught the bus through to Glasgow Buchanan Street. I arrived in Glasgow, walked through the Buchanan Galleries, caught the Subway to Hillhead and found my way to the Adam Smith Building.

There, all the students, who had already met each other, were congregated in a room, just chatting, and as I walked in they all turned and nodded. I stood next to a couple of the young women who were saying how difficult it had been dropping off their wee ones to nursery. One of them said, 'It's really upsetting, it's the first time I've left my wee girl.'

I said, 'Yes, I know. I dropped my granddaughter off last week and felt quite upset,' then walked away to speak to the tutor. As I moved out of reach, I could hear them whispering, 'Did she say granddaughter?'

I just smiled to myself. Pretty much everyone in the cohort was the same age as my kids. Then one of them came up to me and said, 'Sorry, did you say granddaughter?'

I smiled at her and said, 'Yes, I have two grandchildren and four children. My two daughters will be getting married soon.'

There was complete silence for about two seconds, and then they all started asking me questions – why was I doing this course? How had I managed to get on it? Who did I work for? What did my family think? Most of them started comparing me with their own elder family members. It was quite something in our culture for an older woman to suddenly turn up at university, and there was a long discussion about how they would address me. I was quite happy being addressed by my name, and eventually managed to persuade them of this, but there were times when they would call me 'Aunty Trishna' just for a laugh, and to allow me my place as an elder.

I was exhilarated just by being there – I had no idea what was to come or how I would learn in this new environment. I had left school nearly 40 years before, but in my head I returned to that space and the smell of the school just came back to me. I was in for a shock when we were given our list of books to read and asked for email addresses so the tutor could email us information. I didn't have a personal email address – there was a computer at the office, but there was no way I was going to be sucked into emails and be hooked to a box all day. No thank you! People could just write to me.

Everyone wrote down their emails and handed the papers to AK. I decided to speak to her and let her know that I would be corresponding with her in the ordinary way. She just looked at me, then threw her head back and laughed, and in her American drawl said, 'You kidding me, girl?'

I said, 'No. I don't have an email address and I don't want one,' and she said, 'Look, I'll create one for you, and you'll have to use it.' So my email address was created by my American tutor and I still use it to this day.

I knew that my placement was fully funded, however I didn't know we could apply for travel expenses also. Being unsure and not wanting to look stupid by asking too many questions, I decided just to travel by bus so I could keep my travel expenses low. It all started well, and for the first two weeks I felt pleased that everything was going to plan.

I was given my list of books to buy or borrow from the university library. When I looked at the reading list, I was taken aback – I'd never heard of these people, and all the books looked really boring, just totally out of my normal range.

Off I went to speak to AK again. I said, 'I can't read these books, do I have to read all of them?' She asked me what kind of reading I did normally and I said, 'The usual stuff, Mills and Boon, *Woman's Own*.' – I bought *Woman's Own* every week without fail.

She looked at me and said, 'Once I'm finished with you, you will never pick up a Mills and Boon or *Woman's Own* again.'

I have to admit she was right – I've not been near either of these since 2005! That day in AK's office, I couldn't have imagined the bookshelves I have now – full of biography, philosophy, Sikh history and feminist writers.

Things changed at work, too – within two weeks of my starting university, the manager at Sikh Sanjog realised that I was the main link to the women in our community. She contacted me and said I'd have to work my two days in the office and go to university in my own time. Which meant I'd go into the office on a Monday, on a Tuesday I went to university, Wednesday was study day, Thursday back in the office and every second Friday was also university.

So, every Tuesday and second Friday I travelled by bus from Edinburgh bus station to Glasgow bus station. I'd get off the bus in Glasgow, cross the road into the Buchanan Galleries, walk through, get out, catch the subway to Hillhead and walk up the hill to the Adam Smith buildings. I never went into the shops or wandered around – I was robotic! Everybody would ask, 'Did you do any shopping? Did you go for lunch?'

The answer was always the same – 'No.' In some ways I was just so grateful that I'd come this far, I wasn't interested in doing anything else – I just needed to go and come back.

Then I was given the work plan which included things like writing an essay. An essay? The most I remembered about this was 'composition' or 'dictation' in school, where the teacher read out passages and we wrote them down, or something in that vein. Then it got worse, because I'd assumed that lessons would be like school, where you sat in the classroom and the teacher taught you! It soon dawned on me that I had absolutely no idea of what I had signed up to. It was really daunting and I was beginning to worry. I didn't know the first thing about writing an essay, and all the handouts and information seemed like gobbledegook!

I was at my sister, Ashan's, house and her friend was visiting. I told her about my new-found venture and how I was worried about the essay writing, and she immediately said, 'I used to teach, I can look over your work and help you.' Yes! I thought, there is a God and he's hearing my prayers.

Once the first semester was properly underway, I started to get my head round what was expected of me. My understanding of university life became clearer, but things on the home front were pretty chaotic at times. I did everything I could in terms of housework, family events, community events and work life, and also started to plan for Radha's wedding, which involved buying the dowry, planning the engagement and pre-wedding events and preparing the menu. Johnny and both my daughters were allocated tasks, so I could have some room to study.

But then Ashan's friend, who had agreed to read over my essays and support me, called to say she was moving to England so would no longer be able to help. I remember walking home from the office feeling really low. My next-door neighbour, Ewan, saw me and said, 'What's wrong? You're not your usual cheery self today.'

I said, 'I'm just gutted. I've started uni and don't have a clue about essays and the lady who was going to help me has moved.'

He looked at me and said, 'Don't worry, just email them to me. I'll proofread them for you.'

Although Ewan and his partner, Martin, had lived next door to us for over five years and we were on really good terms, I had no idea what they did as jobs. It turned out that they were both professional proofreaders! My doubts about this university caper were beginning to disperse again, and for the next three years, Martin and Ewan read over each of my essays and corrected or highlighted my mistakes.

My first work-linked essay had my tutor calling me in for a meeting, as she was deeply concerned about some of the things I'd written about. To her there seemed to be clear indicators of discriminatory goings-on – and that was putting it mildly, she said. I explained to her at length that this was just normal, and I was adamant that no-one in my workplace was 'like that'. Again, that American drawl, 'Girl, you are going about with your head in the sand.'

Over the next three years, AK would help me to see the environment in which I had worked for two decades in a completely different way. I would learn about feminist theory, and realise that within my own workplace there was discrimination going on that I was not even aware of. I would come to understand that I had been delivering real community development work without ever having a degree. And I would begin to perceive the many layers of covert discrimination that I did not want to believe existed in my world.

It really was the best three years of my life – and yes, I did throw my mortarboard in the air when I graduated!

10

Widowhood

Johnny died on Friday, the 5th of February, 2016 at 9.30 a.m., at home in Craigentinny Avenue. He was diagnosed with pancreatic cancer on the 1st of April, 2015 and from the minute he was diagnosed, he went downhill. The doctors gave him a year to live, at most. He came home and started crying, lying on the sofa. We all sat down with him on the sofa and cried. He stopped drinking from that day on. How desperately sad it was that it took him to be handed a cancerous death sentence before he would stop drinking.

During the following ten months, Johnny was given both conventional Western treatments and alternative medicines. But nothing worked and I could only watch him slowly disappear in front of my eyes. Each day we would say, 'I love you,' to each other, morning and night.

Over the 41 years that we were married we went through some terrible times, but there were good aspects to our life as well. I've kept, and look at from time to time, all the cards he gave me over the years for birthdays, St. Valentine's Day, Christmas, Mother's Day, anniversaries and they all have his handwritten words. Maybe it was his passing that enabled me to see how much we loved each other. We couldn't have had the interludes of good times if we hadn't. It just took me a long time to understand that everyone is an individual and not everyone can show their love in the way that I wanted. But in those cancer-filled last months, Johnny repeatedly said he loved me, even at the end, the day before he died.

On one occasion, when our youngest son was giving him breakfast at the hospice, one of the nurses came in and Johnny perked up and spoke to her. I said to him, 'Why can't you smile at me like that?' and our son said to him, 'You love Mum, don't you, Dad?' and he said, 'Of course I do.'

Two weeks after he died, I was lying in bed and I cried myself to sleep. I had a dream in which I saw him standing at the side of the bed, then he came in beside me and held me in his arms. I started to cry and say, 'Why couldn't you have just kept on taking the medicine?' He said, 'Which one?' and I said, 'The powder one.' The next minute I woke up, crying out his name.

I think everyone who knew how much his depression created havoc over the years thinks I was forgetting that, making a saint out of a sinner. That was not the case. I simply knew that we were true soulmates, which was why we could still say, 'I love you,' every day and mean it. We were like chalk and cheese, yet we had a real, deep love. I don't think I will ever be able to explain it.

Later, I had another dream in which Johnny was standing behind me and I had the sensation that, if he sat on the bed, I would get a fright; I was waiting for his weight to depress the bed. Then he was holding me in his arms, still from behind, and I didn't jerk or feel the need to cry. He said, 'Don't worry, I had to go then.'

We then moved into the room where all my children were, sitting in a row. He had one of them in his arms, in the way he used to do, in a hold so he could tickle them. Then he said, 'I had to go, it was getting too much, even the prescriptions weren't working.'

I woke up, startled, and thought I would be crying, but what I felt instead was a complete inner peace and a feeling of a load being lifted from my heart and chest. It was hard to understand, but I felt as though I was normal again and I knew, with absolute certainty, that he was with me then and always would be.

*

In May 2016 I went to the Bramha Kumaris Global House, London because I had been nominated for an award commemorating the 100th birthday of the spiritual head of this organisation, Dadi Janki. The award, called '100 Women of Spirit', was given to those women who had brought spirituality into their work on a daily basis. But, on a personal level, the most significant thing that transpired from this event was my leaving it with a great sense of serenity, as though a heavy load had been lifted from me. I had gone there feeling heavy, tearful and deeply upset, an inner turmoil seething in me, still asking why Johnny had died and left us. But there was something special about that event, or that place: I came away from it at peace.

*

Three years after Johnny's death, I was sitting by the window in Miro's café on Portobello Promenade, having a herbal tea. I was dressed in trousers and a top, so that I didn't look like a widow to anyone seeing me. I had not been well for the past few days so when I woke up that morning I thought, 'I have to get out of here.'

For three years I had been trying to come to terms with the loss of the one person I loved more than life itself, and I had been thinking a great deal about the word 'widowhood' and what it entailed.

When I looked at all my colourful clothes, scarves and saris of reds and pinks with beads and gold embroidery, they reminded me of him because he had brought them back from India for me. Everyone would comment on his good taste. I didn't need to tell him what I wanted, he would pick out his choices and send me photos of the clothes and matching jewellery that he was bringing back. But when I looked at all this finery, I would think of the word 'widow' and my heart would fill with pain. All the colour had drained from my life. This mourning was not done as part of the cultural expectation, normal in eastern cultures. My heart and my head were clear. I didn't want to look at them because he was not there to say to me, 'You look beautiful,' in this sari or that piece of jewellery. So, I discarded everything except the pearl necklace set that he gave me 30 years previously.

But when I tried on the pearl necklace, a couple of times, although it did look beautiful, I had to take it off because I didn't want to look beautiful any more. Yes, I needed to look presentable and elegant because I knew he would want me to. But if I dressed exactly the way I had when he was here, I wouldn't be able to look at myself.

When I looked at other women who had been widowed, the only things missing from their 'look' were the lipstick and the red dot 'bindi' on their forehead, otherwise you couldn't tell that they were widows. This was just an observation, not a criticism on my part.

When others commented disparagingly if a widow was seen to be 'dressing up', I would go to their defence. After all, they needed to continue with their lives, and without a partner to help them shoulder the problems and issues that would inevitably arise. But now I was one of those left-alone, left-behind women and I was so confused. I couldn't bring myself to go on behaving in the way I had before Johnny's death. My whole being had changed and I was never again going to be that same Trishna who had been one half of Johnny and Trishna.

I realise now that my heart is broken. I loved him so much and he left me halfway through our lives. All our plans and dreams of retiring, of spending six months a year in India, six months in Edinburgh, all gone. Ten months of cancer wiped away a life of forty years together. In all that time my love for him stayed the same as it was the day I found out in 1973 that I was to marry him. I couldn't change what he could become when the depression took hold. We had no understanding or concept of Post Traumatic Stress Disorder and I couldn't do anything except cry. It wasn't diagnosed until two years before he passed away. I used to think no one could possibly cry as much as me; I think I cried so many tears, at times I wondered if I would have any left.

*

What do people expect from widows? We have two options. We can maintain a constant front of cheerfulness so that other people don't have to deal with our grief. However, this attitude upsets me because then I feel guilty – am I forgetting Johnny? Am I now able to enjoy life, knowing that he's not here?

Alternatively, we can show our true feelings, express our grief. But then we risk being diagnosed with depression by the doctor, family, friends and colleagues. We become someone that other people want to avoid, seen to be just hanging onto their grief for the sake of it instead of moving on. But what does 'moving on' amount to? In my case, I fill my days doing lots of trivial things: shopping, cleaning, buying things that I think I need, throwing things away that I think are clutter. I have even taken up gardening which I enjoy because it tires me out.

I would look at all the things that Johnny had accumulated during our life together. Although they belonged to Johnny, I recognised them to be just empty, inanimate objects. I would open his side of the wardrobe and look at the shirts, suits, jackets, coats, socks, tee-shirts, all hanging up.

Those moments did give me some closure, but then I'd be consumed by an overwhelming anger and hurt, especially hurt. Why did this happen? Pancreatic cancer. I had never heard of it, yet it came and took Johnny away from me and made me a widow. He was my soul, and the pain of losing him will never go. Going back home to the silence of an empty house is a pain that only the bereaved know.

In Indian culture, the widow is expected to wail and scream, tear at her hair and beat her breast. All jewellery is removed and she wears a white veil to signify all loss of colour in her life because her husband gave her life colour – and now that he's gone, so too has the colour. The widow's parents will, during the course of the days leading up to the funeral, give her a set of white clothes. They were the people who dressed her in red when she was a bride and now, they are the ones who remove the colour from her costumery by giving her this set of white clothes. These are worn only the once, at the funeral, and are then discarded.

These traditions are steeped in Hindu culture and our community lived by them. Both Hindus and Muslims regarded women as inferior and a man's property. Women were treated as mere chattels whose only value was as a servant, or for entertainment. They were considered seducers and distractions from man's spiritual path. Men were allowed polygamy but widows were not allowed to remarry but encouraged to burn themselves on their husband's funeral pyre (sati). Child marriage and female infanticide were prevalent and purdah (veils) were popular for women.

These were the actions that showed you cared or loved the person who had died. Even if that person had made your life a misery, these rituals must be observed. This ritual was condemned by the founder of the Sikh religion, Guru Nanak, and from a young age, as I began to read from the scriptures, I understood these were meaningless actions which not only added to the stress and pain but also made women feel so useless.

I have, over the years, observed this tradition still being practiced and the pain and anguish of the widows, both old and young, being put through this ritual. As though the loss of the partner was not enough to endure. I would discuss with the females in my family the fact that this is not something we as Sikhs should be doing, it goes against the teachings of our religion. Why do we continue with this awful ritual? And then I gradually stopped attending funerals, or at least staying for that part of the funeral service. I felt I couldn't do anything to change it and people have continued with it even to this day.

Little did I know that my day would come so soon but, when it did, I stopped this wretched ritual from happening to me. I remember the females in my family standing about in huddles whispering to each other. They knew my views on this but they still had to perform their duty. So I watched and listened and then I walked into the room where they all were and said, 'I know what you are discussing, but don't even think about going out to buy me a white suit. I am widowed, I know this, but I don't need you lot buying me a white suit which I'm going to have to throw away once I have worn it, to show the ritual has been completed. And I'm not going to have my children and grandchildren watch me going through this ritual just to please the community.'

There was a stunned silence. I walked out of the room, sat down in my bedroom and cried. I could hear everyone murmuring and saying things like, 'She should do this, it's the way we do things,' 'What will people say?' 'Just leave her,' and so on. Then they stopped.

Six years on, there are still days when I want to scream, smash things up, throw things against the walls, beat my breast and cry so loudly that God should hear me, but I don't. Instead, I just write it all down in my diary.

In those early years of widowhood, I would sometimes look around my bedroom. I'd kept it just as it had been when Johnny was still with me. The books there were all mine – he read, but not in bed. When I took out a book to read at night he would sometimes say, 'Are you going to read that?' And my reply would always be the same,

166

'No, I'm going to eat it!'

But now there was no husband sitting on his side of the bed. Yes, I still had his tartan scarf and grey woollen tammy hat hanging on the bed post, but he wasn't there to wear them. Sometimes I forced myself to feel the emptiness but it was wasn't always easy to do, so I would close my eyes and then I could see him, hear his voice.

That is what a widow is: a lost, lonely person who constantly has to keep up a pretence of coping from day-to-day so that those around her can continue their lives normally without feeling guilty. Day after day, I would pull myself together, get dressed and go to work. If I happened to say to anyone how I was really feeling, I heard the same old phrases time and again – you're so lucky to have work to go to, to have so many friends and family there for you. You're lucky your husband was so supportive while he was alive, allowing you the freedom to be yourself. I listened to all these clichés but I learned not to respond to them. I kept up the pretence of acknowledging their kind words of support, of coming to terms with my loss, of being grateful for small mercies. And, in truth, I was, and I thanked God daily for my circumstances, which could have been much, much worse. The day-to-day reality for me and anyone else who has lost a soulmate was knowing that it would be very easy to slip into depression, desolation and despair.

I once read an interview given by a famous actor during which he was asked, 'Are you a lone wolf?' I then realised that I had, indeed, developed into one. I used to be very gregarious, the 'life and soul of the party', the one whom everyone depended on being around to feel alive. I had become more comfortable in my own skin, more reliant on myself. Like most people, I had hundreds of acquaintances, but only a few of these were friends that I could totally trust, people who tried to understand me as an individual. And, sadly, as my widowhood lengthened into years, I noticed that my phone became more and more silent – this, the landline that rang at all times of the day and night when I was a wife, which used to prompt my husband to say, on many an occasion, 'Are you going to come to bed at any time, do these women not know what bedtime is?'

I think the silent phone and empty house, living on my own, is what made me realise most how people – friends, family, acquaintances – fall away when bereavement comes. They can't deal with the fact that this person, this widow, will never be the same person again. No one notices that you make no comment when the conversation becomes about husbands, they just continue as if you're not there or expect you to take part. I have found that to be the most difficult and painful part of my widowhood. In some ways I have accepted this, knowing that at least I have created a safe space for women to share their stories, their feelings of good and bad experiences. These spaces that we, the women of the Bhat community knew existed for other women but not us, now we have our own space.

Above: At Sandhurst for the launch of the book *Saragrahi* with Rajvinder and Jeevan

Right: Elsie Inglis Hidden Heroines Award, late 1990s

Above: May 2021 Holyrood Palace during the pandemic

Below: Holyrood Palace

Below right: Me and Nicola Sturgeon, Scottish Parliament

Above: Buckingham Palace with my OBE

Right: Receiving my OBE from Prince Charles

Above: Cafe opening at the Acorn Centre, Leith

Middle: 25th anniversary celebration of Sikh Sanjog at City Chambers, Edinburgh

Below: The future of Sikh Sanjog

Above: John Swinney with Sikh Ladies

Middle: Leith Walk Flag Parade

Below: The first ever Sikh Bagpipe Band in the world to be in the World Bagpipe competition held in Glasgow in 2015. They were from Malysia and we hosted them at our Cafe on Leith Walk

Above: Becoming an official member of The Leith Rotary Club

Below left: Me in full flying gear at RAF Leuchars

Below Right: 'Brother' Gareth

Above: Trishna with
Paul Hollywood

Below: Trishna with
Madhur Jaffrey

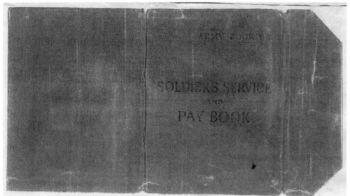

**Puran Singh Pall
Royal Pioneer Corps
British Army Reserve 1944**

Above: My dad and his passbook

Left: My grandfather, Babu Jiwan Singh Pall's visa for Saigon 1930

Above: My traveling grandfather's driving license, issued in Northern Ireland 1951

Right: 1988, India. L-R me, my mum's sister, John and his aunt

Below: John's maternal granny

EVENING NEWS   www.edinburghnews.com   TUESDAY, APRIL 2, 2002   9

Grandson's tribute as pioneering Sikh settler dies in city at 105

REMARKABLE: Mata Ji

ONE of the first Sikh women to settle in Edinburgh from India has died aged 105.

Mata Ji Tej Koursingh passed away peacefully in the city's Victoria Hospital last Thursday.

Mata Ji first came to Edinburgh from Pakistan in 1945 with her husband, Inder Singh, and moved into Springfield Street, Leith, later moving to Elm Row.

Today, her grandson John Singh revealed the family needed a DNA test to find out how old she was. He said there had been no such thing as a record of births in India at the time his grandmother was born and she had forgotten her age over the years.

"She was the most remarkable woman I knew and her memory was fantastic. She was independent and strong until the day she passed away.

A DNA test was carried out and family were astonished to be told she was 105.

"She loved fruit and jelly and had never touched alcohol in her life and,

happened in Pakistan when it was still a part of India and the military movements and she spoke about the past often but over the years it became difficult to remember her age so we asked the hospital if they could help and they obliged."

up until a couple of years ago, she was still able to climb steps up to three floors, so we were a bit surprised to find out she was actually 105."

Mata Ji became a widow in 1959 and spent her elderly years looking after her extended family, which includes 17 grand-children and 55 great-great grandchildren.

Mr Singh said his grandmother was well-known in the Sikh community

in the Capital and across Scotland. "We have had so many calls and cards from people that she knew across the country. She lived for her family and will be sadly missed."

Her family have arranged for a horse and cart to transport her body to the Sikh Temple for her funeral today where mourners will be able to pay their last respects before Mata Ji is taken to Warriston Crematorium for a service there.

Above: 1971. My dad at a rally

Below: My dad and grandad,
Shepherd's Bush, late 30s

11

Life goes on

An intellectual loves truth, desires honour, aims for tolerance, collides with doubts and suffers from continuous struggle with instincts and passions. I need an hour when I can escape through the embrace of society from the vexation of life, then I feel reinvigorated, enthusiastic and youthful, ready to fight on for another 20 years. (Origin unknown)

There's a brilliant book by Helen Clark and Elizabeth Carnegie, called *She Was Aye Workin': Memories of Tenement Women in Edinburgh and Glasgow* – and in some ways, I feel that what I've tried to do here is give a glimpse of a parallel perspective. In her introduction to *She Was Aye Workin'*, Elaine C. Smith says, 'The history that we have been taught at school, in books, on radio and television is not the history of everyday, and that for me is very sad. The real history of the way we have lived has disappeared for Scottish women... It is very distressing to feel that what women have contributed throughout their lives has been largely ignored by conventional history.'

But for women of the Sikh community born in Scotland, the 'real history' hasn't disappeared, because it has never been recognised or acknowledged. In conventional history, we were taught about kings and battles and black people and brown people and the Empire, but not about the Partition of India. We had to piece together our mothers' journeys to this land. We have read about it from other

179

Sikh people's perspectives – both male and female – we've learned about their lived experiences and their history. But the history of the women from the Bhat Sikh community has never been written about. This has been my attempt to share some of it with you: the story of these remarkable, invisible women who have lived amongst you for 75 years. Many of whom have lived and died, known only as 'that wee Indian woman who lived along the road'. They had lives and felt pain and were always at the mercy of invisible internal cultural nuances that shaped their whole lives without giving them a choice.

Elaine C. Smith's introduction goes on: 'This book goes a long way in documenting and celebrating the lives and history of Scottish women. The book is about women of the tenements in both Glasgow and Edinburgh.'

And in exactly the same way, my book is about documenting and celebrating the lives and history of the women from the Bhat Sikh community, who also lived in those tenements, side-by-side with white Scottish women and families. Those families were our neighbours and friends, but our stories were very different behind closed doors. There were similarities, of course, but in other ways it was like being on another planet when the door closed behind a Bhat Sikh woman.

This is just my story, but I hope it helps to change the narrative. Our women have made history in Edinburgh, and it's time to speak up, to be heard and seen – not only in wider society, but in our own families and communities too.

I know we have a very long road ahead of us but I am sure that if we continue to show the same commitment that has been shown in the past, we can only go forward. (Origin unknown)

Acknowledgements

Writing a book about the story of your life is a surreal process. It would not have been possible for me without the people in my family. I want to say a special thank you to my late husband, Harbhajan 'Johnny' Singh for his constant acknowledgment and support in his own inimitable way – 'You do it, you write the book!', without which I would not have reached this stage of actually publishing A Silent Voice Speaks.

I want to thank my children for having faith in me. It is because of their ongoing support that I have a legacy to pass onto my family where one didn't exist before. My sons,Rajvinder and Dilal, daughters, Radha and Neelam, daughter-in-law, Sharon, sons-in-law, Hari and Amardeep and grandchildren, Jeevan, Amahn, Mira, Dhillon and Karanveer.

My dearest friend, Sheila Dhariwal,my constant 'go to' person for nearly 50 years. My friend, always there to hold my hand and give words of encouragement throughout my life's ups and downs in Edinburgh. Always in the background, giving me strength and challenging me when needed, making me believe in myself. My advice to everyone is always have a 'best friend'.

To my friend, Hilary Jones, who introduced me to her husband, who became my honorary brother, Gareth Jones. Without his help this book certainly would not have transpired.I thank you for typing every single page of my 'writings' and then going through them with me, page by page. We started in late 2018; you were so patient and made me think about what I had written in those hundreds of pages over nearly three decades which you eventually whittled down to version 14! At which point you said, 'Trishna, it's ready to go.' I thank you from the bottom of my heart.

My thanks to all of you who have been part of my journey and at times have, without knowing it, given me the strength and encouragement to keep going. My family: my brothers, Gurdev, Subash, Gadraj and Chander, my sisters-in-law, Ravinder and Gurcharan. My cousin brothers, Daldaman, Sukwinder, Dildar, Gurbaksh, Gurmale and Luckwinder.

My sisters, Sukhwant and Ashan, my brothers-in-law (Jeeja Ji) Baldev and Jagdish.

My brothers-in-law, Dalvender, Navinder, Harminder, Satwinder, and sisters-in-law, Sheila and (late) Surinder.

My nieces, Prabjote, Satnam, Soma, Virjodha, Santosh and Rajwant.

My nephews, Kirtan, Gurdeep, Punjab, Rajinder, Luckwinder, Dalwinder, Raju, Roshan, Simon, Krishan, Kirpal, Gio, Himmat, Ryan, Diljeet, Amrik P, Gurjeet and Amrik K.

My nephews' wives – Asha, Bechan, Navinder, Rashpal and Gurdeep.

My great-nieces – Aarti, Amrit, Nirver, Nirbhau , Naseeb, Seetal, Harpreet, Khushi, Sukhmani, Jaya P, Neha, Rea, Maya, Simrin and Jaya S. My great-nephews – Simrin, Arjun, Krishna K, Ravi, Gurdas, Haridas, Ravidas, Akaal, Karam, Nihal, Arun and Eden, 'Always in my thoughts, my dear nephew, Kuljit Pall, who shared the same birth date as Amit Rungu's date of passing. Now two souls sharing a place in heaven.'

Thank you to all of you who have been part of my life in helping me to traverse the world of work and learning in so many ways. It may have been over a long period of time or a short conversation, but your words made an impact and that is what matters. The words that made me think that I had something to offer to the world, something to share and ensure that my, 'our' story was worth telling.

Thank you.

Sue King, (late) Sybil Brown, Nita Brown, Jenny McCallum, Mary McKenna, Louisa Gupta, Steve Cochrane, (late) Saroj Lal, Akwugo Emejulu, Isobel Brown, Martin Mellor and Ewan Halley (my former neighbours), Sheena Ramsey, June Sinclair, Maureen Sier, Ali Newell, Sharon Ritchie, Val McDiarmid, Sam Boyce, Margaret Kinghorn, Joan Dewar, Jo Thorne, Tim Maguire, Ben McPherson, Deidre Brock, Kezia Dugdale, Lisa Clark, Charan Gill, Manpreet Makkar and Mary Batten.

Joanna Boyce and Yonnie Fraser for helping me to read my poem, 'Mothers' out loud without crying! Then putting it on our mural, 'Daughters of the Punjab' for others to read.

My Sikh Sanjog sisters, Jagdish, Rani, Jasbir, Sukhwinder, Rupa, Shaani, Rani, Pritam, Davender, Raj, Kulwinder, Shaminder, Satnam, Jaspal, Kirren, Darshan, Balvinder and Sinita.

Special thanks to Clare Cain, CEO of Fledgling Press, for believing in me and my story.

Thanks to everyone on the Fledgling Press team who helped to bring my book to life.

If I have missed anyone, please forgive me. I know I would not have made this journey without all who came into my life at various stages and helped me to get to this point.

I want to thank God most of all, because without God I wouldn't have been able to do any of this.

GLOSSARY

Akhand Path – A special non-stop reading of the holy Granth Sahib by Granthis which takes almost 48 hours.

Amrit – The holy water for the baptising ceremony: the nectar.

Anand Kaarj – Sikh religious wedding ceremony.

Ardas – The prayer or act of praying with the palms together.

Asa-di-var – a collection of 24 stanzas in the Guru Granth Sahib, from ang 462 to ang 475.

Atma – self, innermost essence.

Brahmins – Hindu priests.

Dhadi – 1. paternal grandmother. 2. A professional singer and narrator of Sikh history.

In this book I have used it when I am speaking about my paternal grandmother.

Gatka – a form of martial art associated primarily with the Sikhs of the Punjab. It is a style of stick-fighting, with wooden sticks intended to simulate swords.

Giani – an honorific Sikh title used by someone learned in the Sikh religion and who often leads the congregation in prayers, such as Ardas, or in singing.

Gurdwara – Literally 'the door of the Guru', the temple or place of worship.

Gurpurub – a celebration of an anniversary of a Guru's birth marked by the holding of a festival.

Guru – A spiritual guide or teacher; the title given to the ten great human teachers of Sikhism, and to the Holy Scriptures.

Hukam – the goal of becoming in harmony with the will of God and thus attaining inner peace.

Karah Parshad – made with equal portions of wholewheat flour, clarified butter and sugar, served to the whole congregation after prayer service.

Katha – speech, narration, story, fable pertaining to the lives of the Sikh gurus.

Kaur – Literally means princess. Suffix for all female names, e.g. Ranjit Kaur, Parminder Kaur. Can be followed by family name, i.e. Ranjit Kaur Gill.

Keertan – The reciting or singing of the Shabad with the help of musical instruments, for example ghana and tabla.

Kesh – the practice of allowing one's hair to grow naturally out of respect for the perfection of God's creation.

Khalsa – both a community that considers Sikhism as its faith, as well as a special group of initiated Sikhs.

Khanda – The emblem of the Sikh nation named after the double-edged sword in the centre.

Sangat – The congregation in a Gurdwara.

Raagi – The professional singer of the holy word or the 'shabads'.

Kirpaan – The kirpaan (Sikh sword) is symbolic of respect, justice and authority. A small 6 inch kirpaan, which a Sikh wears, must not be referred to as a dagger or knife.

Langaar – The kitchen that serves free food to all the people irrespective of their caste, creed, colour or status. Where there is a Gurdwara, there is a Langaar.

Maulvi – Muslim priests.

MECCOP – Minority Ethnic Carers of Older People Project.

Palki – the main structure that houses the Guru Granth Sahib.

Pangat – A special seating arrangement or the principle of sharing communal food in Langaar.

Panj Pyaras – The beloved ones; the original members of the Khalsa.

Parmatma – the universal soul.

Pausha – a month of the Hindu calendar and the Indian national calendar; it's the tenth month of the year, corresponding with December/January in the Gregorian calendar.

Punjabi di Rasoi – original name of Sikh Sanjog's social enterprise.

Rehras – Sikh evening prayer.

Sabha – A society or association; 'Singh Sabha' means Sikh organisation.

Sadh Sangat – congregation.

Saropa – a gift bestowed by sangat on behalf of the Guru Granth Sahib, upon someone who deserves the honour by virtue of his or her dedication.

Seva – selfless service.

Shabad – Means word. The 'revealed word' uttered by the Guru; a hymn, a verse from the Holy Granth.

Shalwar-kameez – Punjabi dress for women.

Simran – meditation.

Singh – Literally means lion, a suffix for all male Sikh names, e.g. Ranjit Singh, Parminder Singh. Can be followed by family name i.e. Ranjit Singh Gill.

Vaisakhi (Baisakhi) – The New Year and the Harvest festival of Punjab. Also an important Sikh festival marking the birth of the Khalsa.

Vedic times – 1750-500 BCE.

Vir Chakra – Indian wartime military bravery award presented for acts of conspicuous gallantry.

Waheguru – is a word used in Sikhism to refer to God as described in the Guru Granth Sahib.

REFERENCES

Bance, Peter *Sikhs in Britain, 150 years of Photographs* Sutton www. suttonpublishing.co.uk

Cole, O. W. & Sambi, S. P. (1990) *A Popular Dictionary of Sikhism*

Cole, W Owen *Five World Faiths* [Chapter Five: Sikhism] Cassell Publishers, London.

Charanjit Ajit Singh T*he Wisdom of Sikhism One World of Wisdom,* Amazon

Darshan Singh *Western Image of the Sikh Religion: A Source Book* (Jan 1999)

Dawson, Julia *The Sikh Community Pack*

Gurharpal Singh and Darshan Singh *Tatla Sikhs in Britain* ISBN 9781842777169

James, Alan G *Sikh Children in Britain*, Oxford University Press, London 1974

Lawton, Clive *A Shap Calendar of Religious Festivals* compiled and edited. July 1985 – December 1986

Lyle, Sean *Pavan is a Sikh* Adam and Charles Black, London 1977

McLeod, Hew Sikhism (Amazon)

Naidoo, G Information Pack on some British Cultures Leicestershire Racism Awareness Consortium

Narang, G.C. *Transformation of Sikhism*, 5th edn., New Delhi: New Book Society, 1960

Nesbitt 1980 1981

Rozina, Vizram *Asians in Britain: 400 Years of History* Pluto Press

Sambhi, Piara Singh *Understanding your Sikh Neighbours* Lutterworth Education, Guildford and London 1980.

Singh, Pritam *All About Sikhs* https://www.allaboutsikhs.com/sikh-literature/sikhism-articles/sikhism-dr-pritam-singh/

Singh Sohal, Jay *Saragarhi: Forgotten Battle*

Singh Kalsi, *Sewa Simple Guide to Sikhism* World Religion Series)
Amazon. Paperback ISBN 9781842777176

Wishart, Peter and Ralf St Clair *Multi-cultural Edinburgh – A short background to some of our city's Ethnic Communities* The Multi-cultural Education Centre 1984

Websites

Dtfbooks.com for all information on Sikhism – religion, culture, people, etc. Books and artefacts, etc.

The British Sikh report 2013 https://britishsikhreport.org/british-sikh-report-download-2013/

www.Bhat.co.uk

www.edinburghsikhs.com

www.sikhnet.com

www.sikhitothemax.com

www.sikhsanjog.com

Further Reading

Cole, W.S. and Sambhi, P.S. *The Sikhs, Their Religious Beliefs and Practices* New Delhi: Vikas Publishing House, 1978.

McLeod, W.H. *Guru Nanak and the Sikh Religion* London: Oxford University Press, 1968.

McLeod, W.H. *Punjabis in New Zealand* Amritsar: Guru Nanak Dev University Press, 1986.

Sacha, G.S. *Sikhs and Their Way of Life*, South Hall, Middlesex: The

Sikh Missionary Society U.K.,1987.

Sikh Studies, Parts I and II, Singapore: Sikh Advisory Board 1985-1986.

Singh, Khushwant *History of the Sikhs* 2 Vols., Princeton, N.J., Princeton University Press, 1966.